"There are so many disconnects in [...] on campuses, or in places of employment. *Especially* [...] job retention rates are low, morale is often lower, and productivity suffers. So what can leaders do to nurture an affirming culture in the workplace? My good friend Robert McFarland has written a stellar guide for any employer who wishes to build a biblical model for himself *and* within his staff. I give *Dear Boss: What Your Employees Wish You Knew* a double thumbs-up. It's *that* good!"

Joni Eareckson Tada Founder and CEO, Joni and Friends International Disability Center

"*Dear Boss* is a practical, challenging, and inspiring guide that reflects its author's many hard-fought years of experience. Not only will it help you become more effective as a leader, it will nurture and strengthen your faith as well."

Jim Daly President, Focus on the Family

"In our national obsession with 'leadership' we often forget that great leadership is reflected in the eyes of our employees and team members. That's why Robert McFarland's new book *Dear Boss: What Your Employees Wish You Knew* is a wake-up call to leaders everywhere. Too often, even visionary leaders are disconnected from the very team that can help them accomplish their goals, and Robert's book is a roadmap that points out the potholes on the road to achievement. Buy this book. It will help uncover your blind spots, and provide the answers you may not even realize you need."

Phil Cooke, Ph.D. Filmmaker, media consultant, and author,
One Big Thing: Discovering What You Were Born to Do

"How often have you played out in your mind all the things you wanted to tell your boss? I know I have and that's why I found *Dear Boss: What Your Employees Wish You Knew* by Robert McFarland so intriguing. What I discovered is the fresh concept of ACTIVE LEADERSHIP as a model worthy to study, follow and replicate. McFarland connects the power found in a leader's words and actions and then demonstrates how to use them intentionally to unleash God's best in people. If you longed for a leader who would do that for you and now want to be that kind of leader, then this is the book for you."

Tami Heim President and CEO, Christian Leadership Alliance

"Workplace culture counts and Robert McFarland's research reveals where it matters most: in the daily interactions with employees and staff. This intel is the key for employers to shape their culture to one of honor and trust in simple but profoundly effective ways. I plan on using this in my leadership classes and in my training of executive coaches."

Dr. Joseph Umidi Executive Vice President, Regent University
MasterCoachApp.com

"Robert McFarland's book, *Dear Boss*, offers every leader an opportunity to quickly improve the workplace. I appreciate his survey findings and Robert's encouragement for managers at every level!"

John Fuller Author, *First Time Dad*

"Robert has addressed, in a very clear and concise manner for employers, some of our blind spots. But he just didn't point them out, he gave us clear direction and guidelines on how we can turn our business in to a happy place—one where productivity will skyrocket. Happy, appreciated employees give their best and look for creative ways to improve the business. This occurs even if they don't have an ownership interest in the business. Robert brings it down to the most important aspects of employee productivity—they must feel like they are appreciated and that someone in management will have an open ear to their concerns and suggestions. This book is a must read for any supervisor."

Mike Smith President, Home School Legal Defense Association

"Robert McFarland has been thinking and writing about leadership and administration for many years. *Dear Boss: What Your Employees Wish You Knew* reveals Christian principles that can help any business flourish. Get it; read it!"

Dr. Jerry A. Johnson President & CEO, National Religious Broadcasters

"Successful leaders are intentional leaders. Nothing happens by accident. If your business faces up to the hard questions, you need help to discover the tough, intentional solutions. What Robert McFarland does with this book will help any leader—in business or otherwise—face the hard questions that your people want you to address, and he provides real-life practical solutions that can become the repeated daily habits you develop to become a better leader for your business and in your home."

Dr. Randy Carlson Founder and President, The Intentional Living Center and Family Life Communications

"*Dear Boss* is a solid look at what leadership needs to be to have business teams function and flourish. It is backed by research and loaded with practical advice. It is a useful look at what it takes to be a good boss."

Dr. Darrell L. Bock Executive Director for Cultural Engagement, Howard G. Hendricks Center for Christian Leadership and Cultural Engagement Senior Research Professor of New Testament Studies, Dallas Theological Seminary

"In this book, Robert McFarland applies biblical principles to the 21st century workforce. With jobs consuming much of our time each day, it is vital to explore how God's word speaks truth in this area of our lives."

Tim Wildmon President, American Family Association

"As one of today's leaders, you are undoubtedly facing challenges that have never been seen before. The super growth of technology, a changing marketplace, employees who have vastly different life values and goals than any other generation, the modern 'family' dynamic, and the list goes on and on. Robert McFarland's *Dear Boss: What Your Employees Wish You Knew* gives you solid, biblical models to navigate your way, not just through today's fast-paced business culture but also how to maximize your impact. I think it is a **must read** for today's leaders."

Mike Novak CEO, K-LOVE & Air 1 Radio Networks

"Robert McFarland is passionate about helping organizations maximize their business and ministry potential. In his book, *Dear Boss: What Your Employees Wish You Knew*, Robert challenges bosses to bridge the gap between employer and employees and reveals how. By following the Biblical road map of an 'Active Leadership' paradigm, we can transform the culture of our companies—and watch how families and even communities can flourish. This is a great book, especially for the times in which we live. You will want to read it and hang on to it as a continuing resource as you embrace the 'Active Leadership' paradigm in your organization!"

Rich Bott Chairman/CEO, Bott Radio Network

"I wish Robert's book on management and leadership had been available in my early days in management. It would have shortened my learning curve considerably and would have been a great blessing to those I managed. I highly recommend it."

Jerry Rose Chairman of the Board, Total Living Network

"Robert zeroes in on what every leader must know to lead a successful organization. The reader can take the clear principles he outlines and apply them today to make a positive change in their organization and individual leadership skills!"

Bill Blount President, Life Changing Radio Network

"Too often we can get so busy making a living that we forget how to live. And, since so much of our life is spent on the job, we need the tools to maximize that significant component of our journey. Based on solid research and infused with loads of practical wisdom, Robert McFarland has written a well-balanced guide to help us find a well-lived career. I have been inspired through my personal interaction with Robert and by his regular blogs. Now, he takes that inspiration to a whole new level to help us find greater satisfaction in this thing called work."

Daniel Henderson President/Founder, StrategicRenewal.com
Author, *The Deeper Life: Satisfying the 8 Vital Longings of the Soul*

"In his book, *Dear Boss: What Your Employees Wish You Knew,* Robert McFarland has nailed it in terms of management staff problems in organizations: 1. Insufficient appreciation. 2. Low morale. 3. Feeling of management incompetence. 4. Poor communications. These issues exist even in ministry organizations. Maybe especially in ministry organizations. But Robert doesn't stop short with just listing the problems. He offers strategies for addressing and resolving those issues, strategies that include praise, trust, and transparency. If you're a manager and want to know what your staff wishes you would understand, you'd benefit by reading this book."

Wayne Pederson Global Ambassador, Reach Beyond
Author, *Reach Beyond*

"If you've ever felt suffocated by your role as a leader, Robert McFarland's *Dear Boss: What Your Employees Wish You Knew* provides the oxygen of heartfelt wisdom—grounded in research—to invigorate you and your team."

Danny Yamashiro President, JCCY, Inc.
Host, *The Good Life Radio Show*

"I have known Robert for years, and we have worked together in Virginia to support Christian worldview principles in our Commonwealth. I know Robert's heart, and this book is designed to really help employers, employees, and the working culture of companies of any size. What a timely subject! Robert has hit it out of the park."

David R. Barrett President/CEO, Barrett Capital Management, LLC

"If you are struggling to find stability in your business, this book is a MUST for you! Robert challenges you to examine where you are and then gives you actionable steps. If you apply these principles you will get the results you desire!"

Nathan Tabor NathanTabor.com

"*Dear Boss: What Your Employees Wish You Knew* is an amazing book filled with information that will be relevant for years to come. From practical insight to emotional intelligence to developing spiritually, all who read it will use this resource as a tool for impacting their environment and for building God's Kingdom in the marketplace."

Barbara Lachance Minister, Author and Entrepreneur

"This book should be in every business leader's library. It advocates for change in the workplace and addressing internal issues to foster a sense of family and working together as a team, rather than every man/woman for themselves. Once a company is actively working together for the common good, retention is better, work improves, the financials improve, and it's a win-win for everyone."

Dr. Emmet C. (Tom) Thompson II NCAA Record Holder,
Businessman, Educator, Author, Speaker, Football Coach

"In *Dear Boss*, Robert McFarland has captured the voice of everyday workers who struggle to connect their jobs to something beyond tasks and paychecks. Through intriguing research on core issues of appreciation, morale, management, and communication, McFarland highlights a wide range of practical steps for becoming the boss most workers hunger to have. Whatever kind of employee you are, this book will challenge you to imagine what "next-level" leadership might look like where you work. Reading this book is worth your time."

Chuck Proudfit President and Founder, SKILLSOURCE® Business Builders

"*Dear Boss* is a book I wish CEOs, entrepreneurs, and leaders of every field would read. Never have I seen such an effective job done in documenting how character shapes leadership and determines outcomes. With fresh research, inspiring examples, and practical steps to action, the author has created a work that is unique and beneficial for readers at all stages of life and leadership."

Dr. Alex McFarland Director, The Center for Apologetics and Christian Worldview,
North Greenville University (South Carolina)

"There is a lot of powerful and practical information to help you more effectively lead your organization. This a great resource to help you improve your work culture. You'll want not only to read it, but to apply it."

Tim McDermott President/General Manager, KSBJ-FM (Houston, Texas)

"Too often, men and women in leadership assume they know what their employees want and need. And too often, that assumption is false. That's where Robert McFarland's important new book comes in. Winsomely, thoughtfully, and gracefully, he calls on leaders to listen, learn, and apply the principles of scriptural truth. McFarland argues that this kind of testimony could be transformative. What he describes could not only make a difference, it could make Christian-focused companies models of what good businesses could be. At a time of great cultural unrest, isn't it time they were?"

Robert Schwarzwalder Senior Lecturer, Regent University
Former Senior Vice President, Family Research Council

"Nagging employee morale issues can remain a mystery to puzzled managers, especially if trust has eroded. In this practical guide, Robert offers insights into why employees disengage and points the way for proactive leaders to move their organizational cultures from sickness to success!"

Dr. Jennifer Epperson Director of Research and Learning, Moody Radio

"*Dear Boss* is more than just a collection of observations from employees. Robert McFarland has written a highly readable and practical guide to developing and actively leading organizational cultures that promote true flourishing."

Kenman Wong, Ph.D. Professor, School of Business, Government & Economics, Seattle Pacific University

"Our society and culture is becoming more polarized than any time in history I can remember. It seems in every setting, sides are being staunchly formed. Robert uses real-life survey responses from individuals to show that the workplace is no exception. Taking the unguarded and private responses of workers about their bosses, he paints a picture that is all too unbecoming—a disengaged employee and an unaware manager. Using practical wisdom that comes from his faith, *Dear Boss: What Your Employees Wish You Knew* is a tool for organizations that are serious about developing leaders who can effectively and consistently create employee engagement at high levels."

Rick Whitted Author of *Outgrow Your Space at Work: How to Thrive at Work and Build a Successful Career*

"I am most grateful to Robert for writing this book. You will be too. There are three elements I appreciated right away. First, his transparency. Transparency leads to deeper understanding. Second, his clarity around the problems we face as leaders—in the workplace, at home, and in our communities; you can't solve the problems without deeply understanding the issues. Third, his definition of and advocacy for 'Active Leadership' is spot on. Thank you, Robert, for deepening my understanding and helping me be an 'Active Leader.'"

Benjamin R. Case President, Case Consulting Services, Inc.

MICHAEL —

May your ability to lead
your team be marked by your
willingness to serve your team.

DEAR BOSS
What Your Employees
Wish You Knew

Matthew 25:40

Robert McFarland

Robert McFarland

Published by Best Seller Publishing

Scripture quotations are from the ESV® Bible (The Holy Bible, English Standard Version®), copyright © 2001 by Crossway, a publishing ministry of Good News Publishers. Used by permission. All rights reserved.

Edited by Alice Sullivan and Catherine Traffis
Cover Design by Steve Fata

Interior layout design by BSP

ISBN 978-1-946978-33-2

To the Lord GOD,
Who gave me the inspiration for this book
and the perseverance to complete it.

To Tamitha, my beloved,
who helped write this book
without writing a word.

Acknowledgments

To Tamitha: Thank you for enabling me to complete this book. I don't know how I would have completed it without your understanding and support.

To my wonderful children: Thank you for putting up with my writing this book and the seemingly never-ending process of editing. I am grateful for your understanding through it all.

To Perry: Thank you for your friendship, advice, and counsel. You told me years ago I needed to write this book. I wish I had listened to you then.

To Gerry and Barbara: Thank you for helping me perceive God's leading and for encouraging me to launch Transformational Impact.

To Alice: Thank you for your editing and guidance in taking this book from a rough draft to something worth publishing.

To Jennifer: Thank you for going above and beyond in helping me polish this book. You will no doubt see your advice in these pages.

To the WPA team: Thank you for helping me gather the research data I needed to write this book.

To all the good bosses I had: Thank you for using your influence to bring out the best in the people who worked for you.

To my Lord GOD: Thank you for the inspiration for this book and for leading me to write it. May you receive all the glory from its publication.

Contents

Introduction

"Perspective is everything when you are experiencing the challenges of life."

—Joni Eareckson Tada

Just three years into our marriage, my wife and I were drifting apart. I had focused on pursuing my career instead of pursuing a relationship with her, and she had focused more of her attention on our new baby girl than on me. Over time, we became more like estranged roommates than husband and wife.

We started the marriage off on a good footing. We had gone to premarital counseling with our pastor. We had been very intentional about making God the focus of our wedding ceremony. We both wanted to follow God with all our hearts. But somehow things still went wrong.

I had become intensely interested in getting recognized by my team leaders. I put in the extra time to make more sales presentations and to make more sales. I wanted to become the best on my team, and I knew that required me to put in the additional time with the company. Since there are only twenty-four hours in in a day, that meant I had less time to give to my wife. She sensed the shift in

1

my priorities and felt my lack of investment in the relationship. She wanted my presence as evidence, from her point of view, that I had our family's best interests at heart. As a result, she let me know that she did not appreciate the amount of time that I was putting in with the company.

My wife, on the other hand, wanted to excel at her own new occupational endeavor, that of being a mother. She wanted to become the best mother she could be. She invested all her efforts in caring for our newborn. She had read books on how to be the best mother, and she wanted to make sure that she put everything she read into practice. From my perspective, all this new attention dedicated to our young daughter made it appear to me that she wasn't as interested in being the best wife. She seemed distant and inappreciative of my efforts to provide for our family. As a result, I made decisions that I thought were the best for the family but were not made in way that reflected her concerns.

We both believed we were doing the right thing. There was nothing inherently wrong with focusing on my career, and there was nothing wrong with my wife wanting to be a good mother. The problem was that we were so absorbed in our own perspectives. I couldn't perceive why my wife thought I was doing wrong, and my wife couldn't perceive why I thought she was doing wrong. Our perceptions forced us into playing the blame game, and neither of us won.

About a year after our daughter was born, everything came to a head. We were on a family vacation at the beach, and I was working. My wife thought we should be spending time together as a family, but I thought I had a great opportunity to do some business with the locals. We had a major argument, and afterwards we had a major realization. We were on a path that was pulling us apart, not bringing us together. Neither of us wanted that to happen. We remembered that we had made a covenant with each other and with God that we would be together until death intervened. At that point, we agreed that we were going to have to make this marriage work somehow.

That started the long, arduous process of refocusing on our marriage. Each of us had to cultivate a tender heart for the other and be willing to treat the other the way we wanted to be treated. We had to change our own perspective from looking at everything from what we personally thought was best,

> *Leaders must take charge in fixing the problems. They must initiate the change they want to see.*

to what we as a team thought was best. Both of us had to put aside our mistrust of the other and make the effort to trust each other. Finally, we each needed to communicate with transparency and listen to what the other had to say without preconceived bias.

We wanted to make our marriage work, and we did make it work. Today, after more than 26 years of marriage, my wife and I are best friends. There is no one I would rather spend time with than her, and vice versa. We still have our issues, but our marriage now is 100 percent better than it was then.

I wish I could say that it was an easy transition from estrangement to marital bliss. It wasn't. It took years to cultivate an appreciation for each other, see ourselves as a team, undo the mistrust, and relearn how to communicate. But I realized two important things from that process:

1) The buck stopped here. I could only change the person in the mirror. I was responsible for the change I wanted to see. Because God had given me the *authority* to lead my home, He also gave me the *responsibility* to lead my home.

I could not place that blame anywhere else. I had to step up or shut up.

2) Neither of us was the enemy. We were on the same team, even though we didn't act like it. We both saw one another as the source of the problem when in fact, we were both contributing to the problem. For the marriage to work, we both had to realize that we were in this together.

Just like the marital difficulties my wife and I had, there is a controversy between team leaders and team members in the American workplace today. In my very first job working in commercial real estate, I saw how relations between management and the union did not go well. My bosses were not perfect, but they did not appear to be intentionally malicious; yet the union seemed to suggest that management did not care about me or my colleagues. Management would explain to us what they were trying to do to improve working conditions, but the union would tell us that wasn't enough. Somewhere, there was a disconnect.

The same situation is happening in companies across America today, even if there is no direct confrontation between management and labor.

- There is no appreciation for the other party. They both see the relationship as adversarial, where one side has to win and the other has to lose. The contributions made by the other party are not validated because they cannot see beyond their own perspective.

- There is virtually no morale. The workplace has become dysfunctional and there is a war simmering just below the surface. Each party is waiting for the other to make a wrong move so they can bring up all the problems the other party is perceived to have created.

- There is mistrust both ways. Associates don't put in their best work because they don't trust their team leaders, and leadership feels that they have to micromanage their subordinates because they don't trust them either.

- There is unhealthy communication between parties. Each side blames the other for the workplace problems they are dealing with, and they are not genuinely open to listening to what the other party has to say.

As a result, morale is in the tank, job satisfaction is abysmal, productivity is compromised, profitability is reduced, and the situation is not getting better. Does this sound familiar?

Much like my marriage in those former days, management and labor are like estranged roommates who are forced to work together. They both feel that they need to hold an entrenched position against the other because neither wants to give up their perception of control—even if they both lose in the process.

Company leadership needs to recognize two things.

1) The buck stops here. God has placed them in leadership not for their benefit, but for the benefit of those in their charge (Romans 13:1-4). Because the leaders have been given the *authority* to lead the organization, they also have been given the *responsibility* to lead the organization. If change is going to happen, they must step up or shut up.

2) Neither party is the enemy. Leaders and associates are both on the same team, even if they don't want to admit it. Both parties have contributed to the problems, and both sides must see their part in solving the problems. To make the company be as productive as it can be, both sides have to realize they are in this together.

Leadership must take responsibility for the situation and admit the mistakes they have made leading up to the present. Even though both parties are at fault, the leaders must take charge in fixing the problems. They must initiate the change they want to see.

Instead of rehashing the same problems in the same way, those in authority must adopt a new paradigm for managing. In fact, the new paradigm should not involve *managing* as much as it should involve *leading*.

Leadership must recognize that the perspectives and behaviors that brought on the problems will not be capable of solving the problems. Those perspectives and behaviors will only perpetuate the problems.

I have worked with myriad organizations in helping them address the best ways to tackle their strategic challenges. My consultancy at Transformational Impact, LLC helps companies and nonprofits envision a preferred future, develop the strategy to pursue it, and create the employee culture to achieve it. To do something they have never done before will usually require a level of thinking that they have not employed before. (To access my personal resources for my one-on-one clients, watch my *What Your Employees Wish You Knew* masterclass, and get your questions answered, visit www.WhatYourEmployeesWishYouKnew.com.)

Using research as a starting point and Scripture as a road map, this book will explore the antagonistic relationship between management and employees in the American workplace. This book blends business insights with biblical wisdom to pave the way for solving today's managerial challenges. Each chapter will contain business applications for immediate use and Scripture references for further study.

To gather the data for this book, I commissioned WPA Opinion Research[1] to ask 589 people an open-ended question: *What is the one thing you wish your boss knew that they might not already know?* This research was conducted online among a nationwide sample of U.S. adults. Multiple online panels were used in the construction of the sample to avoid bias from any one specific panel. The sample included business owners, managers, and employees in a wide variety of industries and ensured representation of gender, geography, education, income, race/ethnicity, and age. The data was gathered September 8-12, 2016, in accordance with industry best practices and standards.[2]

Based on these responses, four themes emerged that encapsulate the problems voiced by employees and faced by management all over the country. These themes involve perceptions of insufficient appreciation, inadequate morale, incompetent management, and improper communication. By exploring each of these themes, we see how they have contributed to the dysfunction of today's workplace and how they can be overcome.

To both address and shift the perspectives and behaviors that have brought about today's dysfunctional workplace, this book offers a solution: Active Leadership. This new model involves implementing a way of thinking that incorporates tenderness, team, trust, and transparency into how management runs the organization. Active Leadership will transform the workplace and enable companies to be more productive and profitable, while becoming happier places to work.

This new model of Active Leadership can be implemented and applied through the process of what is taught, what is celebrated, what is modeled, and what is permitted. By changing the culture of the business, Active Leadership holds the promise of not only transforming companies, but also families, and even entire communities.

Reflection Questions

1. How would you characterize the relationship you have with the members of your team?

2. Why do you think that is?

3. Do you think that the relationship could be made better? How so?

Notes
_____

1 Now rebranded as WPA Intelligence.

2 Responses to research questions can be found in Chapter 1 and Appendix A.

PART I
THE DISTRESS THAT WE ARE IN

Part 1 discusses the scope of the research survey and explains the results. Chapter 1 provides the background for the survey and the demographic breakdown of the participants. Chapters 2 through 5 discuss the four dominant themes from the research by analyzing five representative responses in each chapter.

Chapter 1: **The Research Survey, Its Origin, and Its Findings**
Nearly 600 employees responded to this one open-ended question: *What is the one thing you wish your boss knew that they might not already know?* The responses fell into four major themes.

Chapter 2: **Theme #1 – Insufficient Appreciation**
Employees do not feel appreciated by leadership. They don't feel that leadership has any concern for them as human beings. Instead they feel that they are just machines to be told what to do.

Chapter 3: **Theme #2 – Inadequate Morale**
Employees think that the workplace environment is demoralizing. They may or may not be overworked, but they sense that the conditions there are not conducive to having a strong and healthy team culture.

Chapter 4: **Theme #3 – Incompetent Management**
Employees do not think that management knows how to lead. They do not think their leaders are capable of doing what is in the best interests of the company and their employees.

Chapter 5: **Theme #4 – Improper Communication**
Employees feel left out and forgotten. They do not feel that leadership does a good job communicating important information with them, nor do they feel that leadership is interested in listening to their concerns.

Why It Matters

The research results provide quantitative and qualitative data that point to these four problems facing companies today. By understanding the complexity of the problems, leaders can gain perspective into how their companies can change to address these problems.

CHAPTER 1

The Research Survey, Its Origin, and Its Findings

"Research is creating new knowledge."

—Neil Armstrong

At one point in my formative years, I remember being told of the dangers of wearing ties. Some well-meaning and sincere soul told me that wearing a tie would prevent blood from flowing to my brain. Perhaps that is a reason to this day that I don't like wearing ties.

While ties have traditionally been seen as symbols of leadership among men, this view of the boss having his brain starved of oxygen seems to be a consistent narrative among employees today, based on research conducted by Gallup, Inc. Every year, Gallup releases their *State of the American Workplace* report, which details the dysfunctional condition of workplaces in America. Their 2017 report was no exception. Gallup's Chairman and CEO Jim Clifton summarized it well: "These figures indicate an American leadership philosophy that simply doesn't work anymore. One also wonders if the country's declining productivity numbers point to a need for major workplace disruption."[1]

The Gallup report aligned with my personal experience, even from my first job where I saw discord between management and the union. Today, employees still have a palpable antipathy toward management. I was convinced that it did not have to be this way because of my Christian faith. Let me explain.

When I was in college, I became a follower of Jesus. Up to that point, I had attended church with my family, and had even been part of my church youth group, but it didn't mean much to me. When I went off to college, I told my family that I was going to take a "vacation from religion." That translated into skipping church and drifting from the faith. Despite living the way I wanted, I felt spiritually empty. That emptiness reached a breaking point shortly after my twenty-first birthday, when I realized my party lifestyle left me feeling like I was missing something. At that point, I started searching in earnest for that something.

I had met some people in high school who experienced a radical transformation of their spiritual views. When they accepted Christ as the savior from their sin, they also accepted Him as the Lord of their lives. Their relationship with Christ affected how they thought, how they talked, and how they acted. They said Christ wanted to be included in every part of their lives.

In looking at my life, I realized that my arms-length relationship with God wasn't working. Taking a vacation from religion had resulted in cutting off my relationship with God. I began to realize that God didn't want me to limit my involvement with Him. He wanted all of me.

Going back to my analysis of the relationship between management and the union, I realized that God is not content when we limit the effects of the Scripture to our time in church. God does not recognize a division between the sacred and the secular. He owns everything.

I also realized the Scripture has a lot to say about how we work, how we treat each other, and how we view ourselves. This research survey pointed out the problems that are in the American workplace today, and the Scripture reveals how we can address these problems.

In the fall of 2016, I commissioned WPA Opinion Research to conduct a research survey of 589 adults. Fifty-four percent of them were male, and 46 percent were female. Regionally, 35 percent were in the South, 23 percent were in the Midwest, 22 percent were in the West, and 20 percent were in the Northeast. In terms of age, 34 percent were 18-34, 22 percent were 35-44, 22 percent were 45-54, 16 percent were 55-64, and 6 percent were over 65. (I also asked about their race, total household income, education level, and household size, and the responses to those questions can be found in Appendix A.)

In addition to these demographic questions, I also asked some questions about their work.

Which of the following best describes where you fit in your organization?

I own the business or am part of the senior management team.	12%
I both report to someone above me and have people who directly report to me.	25%
I perform a specific job and report to someone about that work.	48%
I'm not sure/none of these.	15%

I also asked what kind of work they did.

In what industry would you say you work?

Health Care and Social Assistance	11%
Retail Trade	10%
Educational Services	9%
Manufacturing	8%
Professional, Scientific, and Technical Services	8%
Transportation and Warehousing	7%
Finance and Insurance	5%
Accommodation and Food Services	5%
Construction	4%
Local Government	4%
Information Services	3%
Federal Government	3%
Wholesale Trade	2%
Utilities	2%
Real Estate and Rental and Leasing	2%
Arts, Entertainment, and Recreation	2%
State Government	2%
Agriculture, Forestry, Fishing, and Hunting	1%
Mining, Quarrying, and Oil and Gas Extraction	1%
Management of Companies and Enterprises	1%
Other	5%
I'm not sure	5%

Then I asked the 73 percent who said they reported to a boss an open-ended question. To refocus the participants in the study on the question at hand, I framed the question within the context of the communication they have with their boss.

When you think about how you interact with managers, and all the formal and informal communication that occurs, what is the one thing you wish your boss knew that they might not already know?

The typed answers were then collected and analyzed. Other than those who did not respond or were not sure what to say, the vast majority of answers in response to this question fell into four categories.

Appreciation	**17%**
Morale	**15%**
Management	**15%**
Communication	**15%**
Other	4%
Nothing	26%
I'm not sure	8%

The numbers do not tell the whole story. The depth of these concerns is reflected in the verbatim responses from the survey respondents. The raw and honest assessments (fueled by anonymity) show there is a problem facing business leaders today. One particular survey respondent wanted her boss to know "she is a lousy boss." Another survey participant wished his boss knew "That I can adapt to work better than they think." Still another participant wanted to tell his boss "That I am actively looking for other employment."

Over the course of the next four chapters, I will unpack what these concerns bring to light and what they should mean to those in

Your position is not just management—or even leadership— but an agent of transformation.

leadership. Before doing so, I will bring forward a caveat about this survey. I have not investigated the legitimacy of the claims made by the survey respondents. Nonetheless, I submit that the legitimacy of their concerns is of no consequence to this survey. The problems raised are problems that leadership must address for two reasons.

The first reason is that the perception of these associates is their reality. Even if they have the most benevolent, competent leaders on the face of the earth, these survey respondents don't see them that way. Until these team members can see that their team leaders are doing everything in their power to address the issues raised, then leadership still has work to do.

The second reason is that leadership must address the problems raised simply because their team members believe the problems exist. Leadership has not yet sufficiently addressed the issues. It could be that the best way to address the problems is by firing the team members. As far as we know at the time of the survey, leadership had not yet acted to address the concern sufficiently, nor had they yet fired the team members. Therefore, at this time and with the limited information we have, we are forced to assume the problems remain and must be dealt with.

You will benefit the most from reading about this research if you view the sample survey responses without preconceived bias. As you read through the themes that surfaced in this research, it is my hope that you will hear a cry for help and not see a finger of accusation. I realize that you may be jaded by complaints from your subordinates. I suggest that you withhold judgment about what is being said and instead listen to the heart behind the concerns being raised.

If you assume a position of humility and are willing to be taught by these survey respondents, then you may see yourself and your employees in a new light. Your position is not just management— or even leadership—but an agent of transformation. As Jeff Greer and Chuck Proudfit state in *BIZNISTRY®: Transforming Lives Through Enterprise*, "it must be possible, *though not necessarily easy*, to create work environments that glorify God and enable us to help fulfill his larger purposes."[2]

You hold great power to positively influence those in your charge if you are willing to rise to the challenge. You have been given a sacred trust over the lives and livelihoods of people who have been made in the image of God, and that is a responsibility I hope you do not take lightly.

Reflection Questions

1. How much does your faith impact how you lead your team members?

2. Are there any unresolved issues between you and your team members?

3. How could your faith help you resolve those issues?

Notes
_____

1 Gallup, Inc., *State of the American Workplace* (Washington, D.C.: Gallup, 2017); accessed at http://www.gallup.com/reports/199961/state-american-workplace-report-2017.aspx.

2 Jeff Greer and Chuck Proudfit, *BIZNISTRY®: Transforming Lives Through Enterprise* (Mason, OH: P5 Publications, 2013), 36. Emphasis original.

CHAPTER 2

Insufficient Appreciation

"As we express our gratitude, we must never forget that the highest appreciation is not to utter words, but to live by them."
—John F. Kennedy

Appreciation is one of the most deeply held human desires. We all know what great lengths we will go to receive validation from our parents, our teachers, and our bosses. We desire for those in authority over us to accept us for who we are and what we do, especially when we work hard to please them. We are crushed when those whom we desire to please do not notice or appreciate our efforts.

For whatever reason, 17 percent of those who participated in this survey felt their contributions at work were not appreciated by their bosses. Below are five representative responses to the question, "What is the one thing you wish your boss knew that they might not already know?"

1. How to talk to employees with out [sic] disdain in his voice ...
When given the opportunity to say whatever she wanted to the boss, this respondent wanted to point out the boss' perceived tone.

Whether she is accurately perceiving disdain in the boss's voice, it is perceived nonetheless.

This team member seems to think that the boss just doesn't care about her. *Disdain* is a strong word. It brings to mind a revulsion to something thought to be inferior. We do not know the situation(s) that prompted this perception, but the feeling is still there.

Apparently, this employee feels she is speaking on behalf of fellow team members. Based on the survey data, there are others who feel similarly. This is a perception that leadership must acknowledge and deal with.

2. How training works.
This respondent appears to be frustrated by the kind of training offered—or the lack of training—at the workplace. She does not seem to think that leadership understands the specific duties and/or skill sets required to do the job, or what needs to be taught in order to do the job.

Not equipping team members to do the job is a recipe for failure—and possibly even disaster. At knowledge-based jobs, poor training can cause poor results. At jobs where the work is difficult or hazardous, poor training can cause life-threatening situations. At the very least, poor training wastes everyone's time.

We can also infer from this response that leadership does not know that the training needs to be revamped or is not interested in revamping their training. Either way, the solution to this problem rests with leadership.

3. Some conditions employees are dealing with which [sic] are legal but if adjusted would make for a much more positive attitude among employees.
This response suggests that management is not doing anything to change the company to make working conditions better. In fact, it

appears from the comment that the company is doing only the minimum necessary to meet its legal obligations. The boss may be unaware of this concern, or it could be that the boss is aware of the situation

> *Appreciation is one of the most deeply held human desires.*

but will do nothing about it. Regardless, it seems that this employee is speaking for many employees who believe that their bosses are not doing what is necessary to improve working conditions.

We don't know the precise situation behind this response, but management would do well to be aware of employee concerns over working conditions.

4. HOW IMPORTANT IT IS TO TELL PEOPLE THAT THEY ARE DOING A GOOD JOB, INSTEAD OF ONLY COMPLAINING (emphasis original).
Looking at the response in all caps, common etiquette suggests that this person is shouting her concerns. This underscores just how strongly she feels about this situation.

This person's boss apparently does not affirm the team and instead only complains about what they do. While this situation could be real or imagined, usually there is at least a kernel of truth in every complaint, but the boss may be unaware of or even oblivious to how spoken words are negatively impacting the team.

We all can remember hurtful words that bosses have said to us, even years later. While they may not have frequently said the words, if they said them at a time when we were particularly sensitive to what they said, those words can reverberate in our heads as if they were said every day.

5. That I need more realtime [sic] feedback.

In response to the survey, this team member voiced a concern about a desire to receive a response to his work, even if the response is not completely positive. Whether he wants to receive input from his boss to gain validation or to improve his efforts, the desire is for guidance, and to get that guidance in real time. We all know from our own experience that when we did a good job on a project, we wanted to receive affirmation or acknowledgement right then. Not two weeks later.

It is likely this person represents others who want to hear something from leadership about their performance so that they can make some course corrections if needed, or have confidence that they're doing a good job. If they receive no response, it will feel like indifference.

Research from this survey discovered evidence of a crushed spirit in the employees surveyed. The Scriptures say that the spirit is crushed by sorrow of the heart (Proverbs 15:13), and a crushed spirit dries up the bones (Proverbs 17:22). A boss's words will have more impact on the team because of the position of authority occupied in their lives. That position of authority can be abused, even when the boss does not try to do so.

Unthoughtful words can cause much damage. Since you are in a position of leadership, you have a big responsibility to listen to, understand, and encourage those in your charge.

Reflection Questions

1. How much appreciation do you show your team?

2. Do you see yourself in any of these scenarios?

3. Is there anything you think you should change? In what way?

CHAPTER 3

Inadequate Morale

"The best morale exists when you never hear the word mentioned. When you hear a lot of talk about it, it's usually lousy."

—Dwight D. Eisenhower

President Eisenhower understood the importance of morale well. While he commanded the Allied Forces in Europe during World War II, he knew that morale was the intangible force that would drive his troops to do things that they would not ordinarily do. It was imperative that his soldiers trusted him implicitly. Their lives and their success depended on it.

Morale is nearly always discovered by its absence. You don't notice it until you don't have it. An organization's lack of morale can be virtually palpable. We tend to think that we can make problems like morale go away if we pay people more money. That may be true in the short run. However, people will usually determine that the money is less important than a good working environment.

For whatever reason, 15 percent of the employees who participated in this survey thought that low morale at their workplace was their top concern. To summarize the breadth and depth of these concerns, below are five representative responses to the question, "What is the one thing you wish your boss knew that they might not already know?"

1. How to motivate employees ...
In this response, we see someone who wants to be motivated and wants colleagues to be motivated as well, but he doesn't see that motivation coming from the boss.

It is interesting to note what this respondent doesn't say. He doesn't say that he wants to be paid more. Instead motivation from his boss is what is at the top of his mind. We tend to associate money with motivation, and that people will perform better if they are paid better. However, that is not what this respondent is saying.

> *Morale is nearly always discovered by its absence.*

If we think that money will solve motivation problems, then we may learn the hard way that people are surprisingly less motivated by money than we thought. Instead we find there are deeper issues, which tap into our desire for significance that will motivate us more—and that doesn't cost any money.

2. The negative effect her management has on morale and quality.
Here we see a respondent expressing frustration with someone she thinks is a bad boss. However, the problem is much bigger than this employee having a bad boss. The organization's culture has allowed someone to be a bad boss to begin with.

When an organizational culture can condone a bad boss, that is a sign there is a problem in expressing the stated core values throughout the organization. However, it could be that the organization doesn't have any stated values to start with, or that they just don't consistently live them. In addition, it could be that the organization does not care if that manager is getting results, or that the organization is blind to how this manager treats her associates.

Stephen M. R. Covey tells us in *The Speed of Trust* that people don't quit their jobs nearly as much as they quit their bosses.[1] It is paramount for executive leadership to recognize that some of their workforce could be trapped working for a bad boss, and they need to take steps to prevent that from occurring—or to rectify it if they find evidence that this problem exists.

3. I hate my job.
Here is an unfortunate situation where someone shows up perhaps four, five, or six times a week to a workplace only to hate what she does there. To paraphrase Jim Collins in *Good to Great*, she is either on the wrong bus or in the wrong seat.[2]

This is not an isolated case. This situation represents countless other people who don't think that the work that they do matters. They have been left to believe that the time they put in is not accomplishing anything of value. Their company leadership would do well to change their perception—or be left with a workforce that doesn't care about the work product they produce.

4. All of the tasks I'm capable of completing.
This respondent seems to want to help the company work better, yet his abilities have been passed by. Perhaps this person is not as good at his job as he thinks. Nonetheless, this team member wants to contribute more to the team and he feels ignored.

This situation happens in workplaces all over the country, where the systems in place do not allow team members to contribute all they can: A boss doesn't want a particular team member to advance, or executives aren't interested in what team members have to say, or there simply isn't a good way to gauge the team's abilities.

The perceived lack of interest on the part of leadership makes the team members think that their individual performance on the job doesn't matter. As a result, they are less interested in moving the team forward. Those perceptions, whether valid or not, cause them to feel demoralized.

5. How their employees act/work when management is not present. This respondent seems to feel great distress over how his colleagues are behaving when leadership isn't around. While we aren't able to get into his head to understand what exactly is going on, we can see three things right away.

First, this team member recognizes something is wrong; he doesn't know what to do—or is not empowered to do anything— to improve the situation. Second, the behavior of these other employees is affecting this respondent; he feels that others at the workplace are not doing their part, and that becomes demoralizing to his outlook and possibly even his job performance. Third, even if leadership is aware of what is going on, nothing apparently seems to have happened.

The actions of a few can have a strong impact on others. Negative peer pressure can degrade productivity. Inappropriate workplace behavior can leave the company open to harassment suits. Leadership cannot turn a blind eye to this phenomenon, or they do so at the organization's peril.

This research has shown that there are many a "bruised reed" (Isaiah 42:3) in the workforce. If we can listen to the comments that these respondents share and hear the demoralized cries without taking offense, then we can learn from what has not been done well and improve our workplaces.

Reflection Questions

1. How would you characterize morale at your workplace?

2. Do you see yourself in any of these scenarios?

3. Is there anything you think you should change to boost morale? In what way?

Notes
_____

1 Stephen M. R. Covey, *The Speed of Trust: The One Thing That Changes Everything* (New York: Free Press, 2006), 12.

2 Jim Collins, *Good to Great: Why Some Companies Make the Leap … and Others Don't* (New York: Harper Collins, 2001), 41.

CHAPTER 4

Incompetent Management

"Surround yourself with the best people you can find, delegate authority, and don't interfere as long as the policy you've decided upon is being carried out."

—Ronald Reagan

Management is one of those words that everyone seems to understand, yet nobody seems to know what it should look like in action. Therefore, we shouldn't be surprised when we don't like how our managers manage. Besides, it is quite possible they were never taught how to manage effectively to begin with.

We live in a world where the Peter Principle[1] is constantly demonstrated: Team members rise to their level of incompetence. They may excel at what they were hired to do, but they do it so well that they are rewarded with the ability to manage others. However, the skills that brought them *to* that level are not necessarily the skills they need *at* that level. Then they become part of the problem that their former colleagues call "management."

The survey showed that 15 percent of respondents thought managerial incompetence was the biggest concern at their workplace. To give insight into the concerns raised, below are five representative responses to the question: "What is the one thing you wish your boss knew that they might not already know?"

1. What exactly I do and how they interfere with the process.
Here we have a person who believes that leadership doesn't understand what she does. Whether it's real or imagined, the perception is that her boss does not seem to know what's going on, so management isn't able to make sure the team is equipped to do their jobs.

This employee speaks for others who feel that their bosses do more harm than good. Their bosses may feel that it is necessary to be involved in decision making for the team, but not having a solid command of the job compromises their leadership ability.

2. I wish he took responsibility for acting like a manager.
This response is unusual in that this is a complaint that the boss is not acting like a manager. With all the negative views about leadership, it is interesting that this person wants the boss to act more like a manager. This thought brings two observations to mind. First, this respondent has a positive view of what leadership should be: The words used in this survey response suggest that a *manager* ordinarily should exhibit *responsibility*. Second, this person sees that the boss does not inspire confidence in his managerial abilities because the boss does not act like a manager.

A manager who doesn't do what he should can do a significant amount of damage, whether it is intentional or not. Poor leadership by omission or commission is still an instance of the Peter Principle.

3. Ability to be non bias [sic].
Fairness in the workplace should be a key concern of leadership. Playing favorites among certain employees and targeting others for ridicule should not be tolerated, but this survey respondent seems to suggest that this is going on in the workplace.

Lack of fair treatment in the workplace has a demoralizing effect on the team and it has a deleterious effect on the team's view of leadership. It has the potential to create a toxic cultural environment not only because of a boss's behavior but also because of the team's response to that behavior. Team members who are not the favorite will cease to be engaged.

If playing favorites involves a diversity-related matter, the company could have to deal with a charge of discrimination from the Equal Employment Opportunity Commission. Regardless of what the perceived unfairness is, the company would be subjected to bad publicity if the situation were to be posted on social media. Therefore, leadership must be keenly attuned to perceptions of unfairness.

> *Management is one of those words that everyone seems to understand, yet nobody seems to know what it should look like in action.*

4. I know how to do my job so micro managing [sic] is unnecessary.
This respondent feels like his boss is unnecessarily micromanaging performance on the job. His perception is that he knows how to do the job, and that might well be the case. However, the boss doesn't seem to feel that way.

It seems like either this employee does not know what he is doing and should be retrained, or he does know what to do and the manager does not know how to manage. Regardless of the situation, the problem resides with leadership.

Micromanaging can be due to a team member underperforming. In that case, the team leader may feel extra scrutiny is necessary to bring that associate's performance up to par. The key is to appropriately convey that information to the associate. Micromanaging, however, is usually a symptom of insecurity in managers. They scrutinize how the work is done because they lack the larger skills of leadership. As a result, the workforce becomes jaded and not engaged. In sum, efforts at management become counterproductive.

5. People under him are working for the best for the company.
Perhaps the saddest situation evidenced in managerial incompetence is when good work goes unnoticed. That seems to be what this response describes.

This person seems to want to tell the boss, first, that employees want the best for the company, and second, that they are working hard to make that happen. There seems to be two possible scenarios why this employee feels that he wants to share this information: one, leadership may genuinely not know that the employees are working hard to better the company; and two, the boss knows they are working for the best of the company but has not acknowledged that they are. Both scenarios are dangerous to the workplace culture because both will breed mistrust.

This research has shown some traps that the workplace environment can fall into. Even the best-intentioned bosses can have their actions and their motives misinterpreted. Managers will do well to realize that there can be mistrust brewing where there are misperceptions. Where there are misperceptions, fear will proliferate and cause stress and anxiety (1 John 4:18). That fear will come back to bite leadership when employees are stressed and anxious.

Reflection Questions

1. On a scale of 1-10, how good a leader do you think you are? Why do you think that?

2. Do you see yourself in any of these scenarios?

3. Is there anything you think you should change in your leadership approach? In what way?

Notes

1 Popularized by Laurence Peter and Raymond Hull in *The Peter Principle: Why Things Always Go Wrong* (New York: William Morrow, 1969).

CHAPTER 5

Improper Communication

"The single biggest problem in communication
is the illusion that it has taken place."

—George Bernard Shaw

The amusing quote by George Bernard Shaw humorously points out something that is not actually funny. In workplaces all over America—and even in families and marriages—people assume that they communicated something just because they said it. Nothing could be further from the truth.

For communication to happen, it requires someone to say (or write) something, someone to hear (or read) something, and for what they heard (or read) to be understood. Oftentimes messages are said, but not understood—or worse, not even heard. Therefore, communication frequently does not happen.

From the survey, we see that 15 percent of the respondents said that improper communication was the issue of greatest concern with their boss. Below are five representative quotes from respondents answering the question, "What is the one thing you wish your boss knew that they might not already know?"

1. How they are really perceived.
This respondent seems to have a lack of respect for his boss based on past behavior. Perceptions can be tainted because of improper communication. Often, these perceptions are caused by deep-seated misgivings from unresolved issues in relationships, whether personal or professional.

A lack of transparency can cause misunderstandings in communication that lead to mistrust and building up walls between people. This is a difficult cycle to stop because there has been so much bitterness hardened over time between bosses and the people who report to them. As a result, neither party believes what the other party has to say, and the cycle continues.

> *People assume that they communicated something just because they said it. Nothing could be further from the truth.*

2. Details of responsibility sharing with other department teams.
This respondent seems frustrated by a lack of clarity with the boss. It seems the boss has been intentionally or unintentionally vague in communications about responsibilities or has been disinterested in what the teams are doing. Regardless what the exact situation is, communications seem to be unclear.

This employee no doubt speaks for others regarding their frustration with the lack of clarity surrounding their responsibilities. When performance expectations are unclear, then results will suffer because employees don't know what is expected of them.

Without clarity, team members will come to their own conclusions as to what is going on—and that may be completely the opposite of what is actually going on.

3. How to communicate effectively.
This respondent seems to be familiar with George Bernard Shaw's quote because she bemoans her boss's lack of ability to communicate effectively. Even though bosses tend to be the ones to share information, they run the risk of assuming that they have communicated simply because their message was relayed. Bosses will alienate their employees if they do not take the time to verify the message was conveyed and hear what employees have to say in response.

4. That all employees need to be aware of what is going on in the workplace, not just a handful of upper level administrators.
There can be a perception among team members that the team leader is hoarding information, and not informing them about issues that affect them. This respondent seems to think that her boss is not telling them the whole story.

Leadership may be doing this unintentionally. It is possible that they want to wait to share information until they are sure that it is completely accurate. In the absence of facts, however, rumors will start. When people feel there is a void of information, then something will fill that void and it may not be true. In fact, usually it is not.

As a result of the practice of information hoarding—or the perception of information hoarding—team members can come to resent the lack of information. They can also come to resent leadership.

5. That we need to meet at least once a week so everyone can be on the same page.
This response may sound like a desire to waste time in staff meetings, but this person seems to be voicing a legitimate concern about everyone having the same information. It sounds like either

information is being shared in writing or it is not being shared at all. It appears that he senses there is a problem because communication is not shared in person on a weekly basis.

While this situation seems similar to the practice of hoarding information, it is distinctly different. When we talk about attitudes and feelings, words comprise only 7 percent of our communication. Vocal inflection provides another 38 percent, and visual nonverbal communication provides 55 percent. As a result of not meeting in person, most of that communication is not provided and likely is assumed.[1]

This research seems to suggest that your yes must be yes and your no must be no (Matthew 5:37). When communication is poor, then the process of working together breaks down as well. Without that cooperation, a business venture is hampered at the least—and doomed to fail at the worst.

Reflection Questions

1. On a scale of 1-10, how good a communicator do you think you are? Why do you think that?

2. Do you see yourself in any of these scenarios?

3. Is there anything you think you should change about your communication techniques? In what way?

Notes

1 Stephen M. R. Covey, *The Speed of Trust: The One Thing That Changes Everything* (New York: Free Press, 2006), 212.

PART II

ACTIVE LEADERSHIP

In Part Two, we will explore what can be done by exercising Active Leadership to address the concerns discovered through the research. Active Leadership is the intentional awareness of the thinking, words, and actions necessary for you to bring out the best in the people in your charge.

Chapter 6:   **The Need for Active Leadership**
Based on the state of the American workplace, management needs to be willing to change how it looks at managing. Unless the paradigm shifts, the results will continue to be the same—or worse.

Chapters 7-12:   **Paradigm Shift #1 – Tenderness**
Leadership must care enough about their team so they believe that leadership genuinely cares about them and takes an active and ongoing interest in their professional and personal development. Leadership must regularly give praise for what

the team does well and compassionately give constructive feedback to help employees improve. Leadership also must place a premium value on flexibility in the workplace and be willing to change.

Chapters 13-18: Paradigm Shift #2 – Team

Leadership must ensure that everyone understands and identifies with the vision of the organization and subscribes to the organization's core values. Leadership must explain the importance of the work that the organization does to the extent that the employees believe that the work they do matters. Everyone must see that their individual performance is important to moving the organization forward, and leadership must ensure that everyone feels that their colleagues are all doing their part.

Chapters 19-24: Paradigm Shift #3 – Trust

Leadership must inspire their team to have confidence in the leaders' ability to run the organization. Leadership must provide sufficient autonomy for assignments and must empower the team to select the tools they believe are necessary to do their jobs. Leadership must also ensure that they treat all employees fairly and trust their employees to do their best work.

Chapters 25-30: Paradigm Shift #4 – Transparency

Leadership must communicate authentically with the team and ensure that communications with employees are understood by everyone. Leadership must be willing to freely share

information—in person as often as practicable—
and clarify responsibilities so that employees
understand what is expected of them.

Why It Matters

By making these four paradigm shifts from "business as usual" to an
Active Leadership model, you can understand how to remake your
organization through a culture that is more positive, a bottom line
that is more profitable, and a focus that is more transformational.

CHAPTER 6

The Need for Active Leadership

*"Paradigms are like glasses. When you have incomplete
paradigms about yourself or life in general,
it's like wearing glasses with the wrong prescription.
That lens affects how you see everything else."*

—Sean Covey

Senate Minority Leader Everett Dirksen was famous for his rhetorical style, earning him the nickname the "Wizard of Ooze."[1] He sounded like a true politician. One of his more famous lines was "I am a man of fixed and unbending principles, the first of which is to be flexible at all times." However, he is likely best known for this line: "When I feel the heat, I see the light." When Sen. Dirksen would feel the political pressure, he would realize he needed to change how he would vote. When his situation would become untenable, then he would realize he needed to do something different.

Today, business in America is feeling the heat. The perspectives and practices that have brought American businesses to this point are no longer working. Gallup has documented this trend since

2010 in their *State of the American Workplace* report. Based on data collected from nearly 200,000 employees and 31,000,000 respondents through their client database, their 2017 *State of the American Workplace* report found only one third of the American workforce is engaged at their jobs, half of American workers are not engaged, and one sixth are actively disengaged.[2]

American management has produced low productivity, toxic workplace cultures, poor job satisfaction, compromised profitability, abysmal morale, and mistrust between leadership and employees. There is no question that business in America is feeling the heat. The question is whether it will see the light.

This problem has been around for quite a while. Based on Gallup's data, the lack of engagement of the workforce has been around since at least the turn of the millennium,[3] and based on the trends it shows no sign of changing in the near term.

John Mackey, Co-CEO of Whole Foods Market, sees this situation as endemic. "Too many businesses have operated with a low level of consciousness about their true purpose and overall impact on the world. Their tendency to think in terms of trade-offs has led to many unintended, harmful consequences for people, society, and the planet, resulting in an understandable backlash."[4]

The American workplace is not changing by itself, and you cannot expect it to change on its own. If your company is going to change, it will change through your Active Leadership. Change doesn't happen easily. It starts with the willingness to acknowledge that your perspective is not the only one and that it might not lead you to correct conclusions. Change starts with recognizing how you look at the world. Change starts with the ability, as Everett Dirksen said, to see the light.

We all look at the world from a particular paradigm or pattern. It's how we make sense of the world and everything that goes on in our lives. When we realize that our paradigm doesn't work, then we must consider whether we should stick with how we have always done things or if we should make a paradigm shift. When we shift our paradigm, we open our minds to how we could look at things differently.

In a historical context, we know that Galileo's claims that the earth revolved around the sun required a major paradigm shift. Up to that time, everyone assumed that the sun revolved around the earth. It took a major paradigm shift to recognize a heliocentric cosmology instead of a geocentric cosmology.

You deserve kudos for picking up this book and reading this far. It shows that you are willing to change. I believe you want what's best for your company and for your employees, and you are willing to change your thinking to make that happen. I can see you are willing to make a paradigm shift.

From what we saw in the last section of the book, there are four major issues that need to be addressed in American companies. More importantly, these four issues are likely evidenced in your workplace as well. Probably none of these issues have been intentionally practiced in any workplace. However, these four issues have crept into the workplace slowly over time through repeated interactions between team leaders and team members.

1. Team members feel insufficient appreciation on the job. They don't receive enough praise for what they do well, but instead they are told what they do wrong. They don't feel cared about by team leaders personally or professionally. They don't receive enough feedback about how they are doing, and they feel management won't do what's needed to change.

2. Morale is low in the workplace. Employees don't see how what they do fits in with the big picture in the organization,

they don't believe their personal efforts make any difference in the company, and they don't feel that others are doing what they should be doing.

3. Team members are distrustful of leadership. They don't feel that their leaders trust them to do a good job or equip them to produce good work. They don't feel fairly treated by their bosses, and they don't have confidence in their bosses' leadership abilities to run the company.

4. Effective communication does not take place. Associates feel that their leaders are being untruthful or that they're holding information back from them. In addition, they don't feel like they understand their bosses' perspectives or that their bosses understand their perspectives.

It doesn't have to be this way. You don't have to do things the way they have *always* been done. You can make a paradigm shift, and you can change your company for the better. In the rest of this section, you will read about a new model for leadership—Active Leadership. In fact, your Active Leadership is more important than you may realize.

When I say leadership, I mean influence. Leadership is the ability to influence others and affect their actions. Leadership also denotes being out in front and guiding and directing the actions of others simply by being a visible example. Leaders make an impact, whether they realize it or not, simply because they have a platform to change the behavior of their followers.

> *You are in a position of leadership to serve your team. Don't squander it by being merely a boss.*

"Servant leadership," popularized by Robert Greenleaf[5] in the 1970s, is a perspective aimed at leading through serving. The focus is on leading others by demonstrating genuine concern for their well-being. Jesus encapsulated this concept in the Gospel of Mark: "You know that those who are considered rulers of the Gentiles lord it over them, and their great ones exercise authority over them. But it shall not be so among you. But whoever would be great among you must be your servant, and whoever would be first among you must be slave of all" (Mark 10:42-44).

By Active Leadership, I mean leadership that is fully engaged and intentional. Active Leaders think through the impact they want to have—and the thinking they need to cultivate to achieve it—and they deliberately use every opportunity they have to influence their followers to that end. They take their responsibility as leaders very seriously because they realize all their actions have ripple effects.

As a leader, you are the catalyst for the change you want to see in your team. You cannot expect that your team will do what you want them to do on their own. They will want to see your Active Leadership to show them how.

As you lead your team, the Golden Rule should guide your actions: "So whatever you wish that others would do to you, do also to them, for this is the Law and the Prophets" (Matthew 7:12). It is not just about treating your customers well; it goes beyond that. It's about treating everyone in your sphere of influence that way, including your employees, your suppliers, your investors, and the people in your community.

You are in a position of leadership to serve your team. Don't squander it by being merely a boss. Good leadership is not bossing others around. Good leadership is using your mind, your actions, and your influence to serve others.

You set the tone as the leader. Think about what kind of person you want to have working for you. Then act like that person. Be the example of the person you want to have working for you because they will follow if you lead them well.

Do not be so stuck on being a leader that you forget to serve. Lead by example by doing something that you shouldn't have to do, so that others will be willing to do things that they shouldn't have to do. Organizations function because people are willing to subject their own interests to the interests of the organization. When you show you are willing to serve, then you are demonstrating the behavior you want your employees to emulate.

Your Active Leadership will change how you view yourself, your employees, and your company. Through conscious awareness of these concepts, you will begin to look at things differently. With this new lens, you will be able to redefine your role as a leader, and it will redefine how you view everything else at your company.

In unpacking this Active Leadership paradigm, we will discuss four paradigm shifts.

1. Tenderness
Leadership must be willing to treat their employees as they would want to be treated if the situation were reversed. Leadership must view employees as people to be led instead of machines to be monitored.

2. Team
Leadership must recognize that they and their employees are two parts of the same team. Leadership must cultivate a team environment where they abide by the same rules they expect their employees to abide by.

3. Trust
Leadership must be willing to trust their employees. If the employees do not feel that they are trusted by leadership, then the employees will not be willing to trust leadership.

4. Transparency

Leadership must be willing to have open communication with employees. Not only does that mean sharing information freely with employees, but it also means being willing to listen to employees as well.

Through exploring these four paradigm shifts of Tenderness, Team, Trust, and Transparency, you will be able to cultivate a mindset to produce a 4T Culture in your work environment that not only your employees will appreciate, but you will enjoy more too.

Reflection Questions

1. In the terminology of Sen. Dirksen, how much do you "feel the heat" in your workplace?

2. How would you describe your personal paradigm or worldview?

3. How closely does your leadership style match the definition of Active Leadership?

Notes

1 Wikipedia, s.v. "Everett Dirksen," last modified August 30, 2017, https://en.wikipedia.org/wiki/Everett_Dirksen.

2 Gallup, Inc., *State of the American Workplace* (Washington, D.C.: Gallup, 2017); accessed at http://www.gallup.com/reports/199961/state-american-workplace-report-2017.aspx.

3 Ibid.

4 John Mackey and Raj Sisodia, *Conscious Capitalism: Liberating the Heroic Spirit of Business* (Boston: Harvard Business School Publishing Corporation, 2014), 16.

5 Robert K. Greenleaf, *Servant Leadership: A Journey into the Nature of Power and Greatness*, 25th anniv. ed. (1977; reprint, New York: Paulist Press, 2002).

CHAPTER 7

Tenderness

"There is no charm equal to tenderness of heart."
—Jane Austen

After his resurrection from the dead, Jesus appeared to his disciples on the Sea of Galilee but they did not recognize him at first. They had been fishing all night and had not caught anything when Jesus told them to cast their nets on the right side of the boat. When they brought in such a catch that they could not haul it all in, they realized it was Jesus.

After their breakfast of fish, Jesus talked alone with Peter. Although Peter had denied Jesus three times before his crucifixion, Jesus was tenderhearted with Peter. He gave Peter the opportunity to affirm his love for him three times, the same number of times he had denied him. Instead of castigating Peter for abandoning him, Jesus loved him, and Peter devoted the rest of his life to following Jesus (John 21:1-19).

Jesus's treatment of Peter demonstrates the profound impact leaders can have on their followers. Leaders have the ability to help their followers become all they can be. How leaders treat their teams can make a big difference in how well their teams perform.

At the same time, leaders also have the power to destroy their team's drive to perform. The 2017 *State of the American Workplace* report found that only 33 percent of employees in America are engaged in the work they do, and only 21 percent strongly believe that their managers encourage and develop them to excel at what they do.[1]

These are disappointing statistics. While we may be tempted to dismiss the non-engaged 67 percent as just deadwood, we see that 79 percent of employees do not believe that their bosses are encouraging them or developing them to excel in the workplace. With numbers like that, as I stated earlier in this book, leaders cannot simply shrug off the situation as some other company's problem. When four out of five employees do not feel encouraged or developed at their workplace, the odds are that you have people who feel that way at your workplace.

Based on these numbers, the American workplace is not the place where people are being taught that they are valued. Some may argue that is not the responsibility of business. We don't tend to think of companies being places where people are loved and cared for. As Whole Foods Co-CEO John Mackey and Raj Sisodia explain in *Conscious Capitalism*, "people tend to think of love and care as something we only share with our families, friends, or community organizations. This cultural bias comes from the common belief that love and care interfere with effectiveness in the real world. People see the marketplace as a jungle of competition; they fear that businesses that emphasize love and care cannot possibly be competitive and win. In fact, the opposite is true. Love and care are not weak virtues; they are the strongest of all human traits."[2]

Companies can be environments where people thrive. We can produce an environment where people are valued and appreciated. We can produce a workplace where the humanity of employees is affirmed. When employees feel valued, then they will provide more value to the people they serve.

No doubt someone reading this book will think that businesses should only be concerned with profit maximization and on making employees high performers. Some people will always be uncomfortable with this "touchy feely" perspective. However, Mackey validates this "touchy feely" perspective with Whole Foods' multi-billion-dollar annual sales revenue. He and his co-author of *Conscious Capitalism* state that "this way of doing business not only creates a great deal of well-being and happiness for all the stakeholders, but it is also the secret to sustained high performance."[3] Mackey and Sisodia believe the American business model has forgotten that the people that they employ are human beings, and they cannot check their humanity at the workplace door. "In recent years, the myth that business is and must be about maximization of profits … has robbed most businesses of the ability to engage and connect with people at their deepest levels."[4] As a result, people do not associate giving of the best that they are to their place of employment. They are not used to it, and they have not been inspired to reach for it; people cannot give what they do not have.

Businesses would be wise to turn this tide. If they change their culture of business to embrace a Culture of Tenderness toward their employees, everyone wins. Not only will they have happier employees, they will have a more engaged workforce, and they will ensure greater performance from their employees.

In *Conscious Capitalism*, Mackey and Sisodia document through a study of eighteen businesses over a ten-year period that having a purposeful, healthy, and team-oriented culture will produce outstanding financial returns. These are the six points they used to describe the companies in the study.

> First, the companies did not state their goal as "maximizing shareholder concerns." Second, most of these companies pay their team members well and provide generous benefits. ... Third, these companies paid taxes at a much higher rate than that paid by most other companies. Fourth, the selected companies did not squeeze their suppliers to secure the lowest possible price. ... Fifth, [they] invested a lot in their communities ... Finally, they provided great customer value and outstanding customer service. ...
>
> [The authors] found that these companies not only do all those good things, but also deliver extraordinary returns to their investors, *outperforming the market by a nine-to-one ratio over ten years* (from 1996 to 2006). ... [T]hese same companies *outperformed the S&P 500 index by a factor of 10.5 over that period.*[5]

Not only is this Active Leadership paradigm a biblical model for business—as a result of observing the Golden Rule (Matthew 7:12)—it is also a more profitable way to operate your business, as documented by Mackey and Sisodia.

> *People cannot give what they do not have.*

In this section, we will explore what a Culture of Tenderness looks like. In each chapter about Tenderness—and in the subsequent chapters about Team, Trust, and Transparency—I will pose a Culture Health Question to frame the focus of the issue, which ties back to the comments made by the respondents in the preceding chapters. In the next five chapters, we will explore the following five topics.

Caring Produces Tenderness

Leadership must care enough about their team that their team members believe their leaders genuinely care about them. If leadership tries to fake this, their employees will know. This sentiment must be from the heart.

Training Propagates Tenderness

Leadership must take an active and ongoing interest in their team members' professional and personal development. Leadership must look at what their employees could be—not who they are today—and be committed to helping them get there.

Flexibility Preserves Tenderness

Leadership must be humble enough to be flexible with their team. Leaders must not cling to the rules and instead be willing to creatively respond to the situation.

Praise Professes Tenderness

Leadership must regularly give praise for what employees do well. Employees will focus on doing good work if they know that their efforts will be noticed and appreciated.

Feedback Provides Tenderness

Leadership must compassionately give constructive feedback to help employees improve. Employees will work at getting better if leadership focuses on helping them to get there.

It is my prayer that in the following chapters you will gain a greater understanding of how you can embrace the humanity of the people in your employ. Through that understanding, you will see how you can bring your employees to a new level of performance and your company to a new level of value creation for your customers.

Reflection Questions

1. In the past, have you been uncomfortable with a "touchy feely" model of doing business?

2. How much have you reconciled your faith with your business leadership?

3. How could you cultivate a Culture of Tenderness at your workplace?

Notes
_____

1 Gallup, Inc., *State of the American Workplace* (Washington, D.C.: Gallup, 2017); accessed at http://www.gallup.com/reports/199961/state-american-workplace-report-2017.aspx.

2 John Mackey and Raj Sisodia, *Conscious Capitalism: Liberating the Heroic Spirit of Business* (Boston: Harvard Business School Publishing Corporation, 2014), 225.

3 Ibid., 299.

4 Ibid., 16.

5 Ibid., 277-278. Emphasis added.

CHAPTER 8

Caring Produces Tenderness

"There is no fear in love, but perfect love casts out fear."

—1 John 4:18

In the spring of 2002, my father's health was failing. He had fought a valiant, six-year battle with lymphoma, and the complications from the treatments were taking their toll. For most of his life, he had been a very healthy man, so it was difficult for me to process that my father's life was drawing to a close.

Three years prior, my parents had moved to the Washington, D.C. area to be closer to my sister's family and to my family. Since we all lived approximately 30 minutes from each other (without traffic), my sister and I had the ability to visit our father often during this time.

My boss was sympathetic to what I was going through. I had only worked for Frank for a little more than a year when my father's health started failing quickly, so I didn't know him that well. Nonetheless, he expressed concern for my father's health and how I was dealing with it. At the time, I did not quite fully understand how sympathetic he would be.

My father died at the age of sixty-one on Memorial Day, which was fitting since he was an army officer. He had been born and raised in the Atlanta area, and his desire was to be buried there. My mother, my sister and her family, and my wife and I with our children all flew down to Atlanta to be with the rest of our extended family. The days leading up to and after his burial helped our family to celebrate my father's life, but Atlanta was too far for our Washington, D.C.-based friends and support network to travel for the service.

When I returned to the office after my father's burial, I notified my colleagues that my family would host an open house for people in the local area to express their sympathies. At the open house, dozens of people came to call over the course of the evening. In fact, so many people came to visit that it was hard for my mother, sister, and I to get to the door to answer it. One time the doorbell rang and I went to get the door. I will never forget the moment I opened the door and saw Frank standing on the doorstep.

By showing up outside of work hours at a low point in my life, Frank made a huge impact on my life and on my career. That simple gesture showed that he genuinely cared about me and what I was going through.

One of the first ways you can demonstrate tenderness at the workplace is to show that you care about your team. One of the respondents from the research survey we discussed in Chapter 2 said he wished the boss knew "How to talk to employees with out [sic] disdain in his voice." That's why the Culture Health Question for this chapter is: *Do employees believe that leadership genuinely cares about them?*

The secret to showing that you care about your employees is the same way you get good employees to come to work at your company—and then stay with your company. The secret is not really a secret. It's treating everyone the way you would want to be treated (Matthew 7:12). In a word, it's love.

When I say the word *love*, I am not talking about a romantic kind of love. I am talking about a New Testament kind of love. The Bible writers used the Greek words *agape* and *agapao* to describe love in a social or moral sense. This is the kind of love that Jesus said we should have for our neighbor: We should *agapao* our neighbor as ourselves (Matthew 22:39).

When you have a positive environment where your employees feel the love—or *agape*—then they will feel that you care about them. This kind of love should apply not just while they're on the job, but for them as a whole person. Just as my boss showed up to express his sympathies after my dad died, acknowledging your employees' humanity in personal situations will go a long way.

Look after your team. Take more than a casual interest in their home life. Be actively concerned about their welfare. Don't think about only what your team can do for you. Think about what you can do for them. If someone on your team is going through a tough time, let them know you are thinking about them. Send them a card. Talk to them at work. Offer to meet with their family. Don't let them feel left behind. They are humans before they are employees.

One of the most loving and caring things you can do for your team is to remove fear from your workplace culture. It also happens to be one of the best investments you can make in your company. As John Mackey and Raj Sisodia point out in *Conscious Capitalism*, companies "that consistently produce high performance gently but firmly synthesize excellence with love and care." They further elaborate on the importance of love in the workplace. "A company built on fear and stress is like a house infested with termites; it may look fine from the outside but it is being eaten away from the inside until one day, it just collapses. When a culture is full of fear, work becomes a painful ordeal to be endured. Unfortunately, this is far too common. People who don't suffer from the Monday morning blues have become a rarity."[1]

Here are three things that will happen if you remove fear from your workplace culture.

1. Your team will feel accepted.

When you replace fear with love in your workplace culture, your team will feel more accepted. They will start to let the walls down in their lives, and they will become more like the people God made them to be.

Fear is not a healthy motivator, but love is. As Mackey and Sisodia explain, "too many leaders continue to believe that fear is a better motivator than love. Fear is the opposite of love. When we are completely grounded in love and care, fear is not present."[2] Fear and love cannot coexist, because love—or *agape*—drives out fear (1 John 4:18).

When you love—or *agapao*—your team, you will help their personalities to flower. When they are in fear, it's as if their souls are starved of sunlight. When they feel loved and appreciated, they get enough sunlight for their souls to bloom. When you have *agape* in your workplace, you will have better employees because they will become more of who they really are. They will be more like the people who you want to have at your company.

The secret to showing that you care about your employees is not really a secret. It's treating everyone the way you would want to be treated. In a word, it's love.

2. Your team will be more innovative.

When you remove fear from the workplace, your employees will be more innovative because they will feel like they have the freedom to offer up new ideas. Mackey and Sisodia write that "[f]ear is especially deadly for creativity. To be really creative, people need to be in a flow state, and fear doesn't permit that to happen."[3]

When you genuinely love—*agapao*—your employees, they will feel the freedom to be creative. They will have more mental energy to think outside the box. And they will be more willing to step out of their comfort zone. When you have love in the workplace, your team will be willing to try new things because they won't be afraid to fail.

3. Your team will do their best work.

Replacing fear with love—or *agape*—is not only an altruistic gesture. It is also a smart investment in the future of your company. As Mackey and Sisodia explain, fear "prevents people from fully self-actualizing and prevents organizations from realizing their full potential."[4] When you have fear in your culture, it's as if your team is running a race with shackles on their legs. When you remove the fear, you take the chains off.

When fear is no longer in the workplace, your team will want to do their best work for you because they recognize that you want to bring out the best in them. By caring for your employees, you will create the environment where they want to give back to you because you have loved them enough to believe in them.

You can do so much more than make a great workplace when you replace fear with *agape*. You can create an environment where people can rediscover who they are and who God made them to be. In the process, you will develop more confident, innovative, and competent employees who will in turn make your company more productive.

Reflection Questions

1. How can you impart a sense of love and caring into your workplace?

2. How can you remove fear from your workplace?

3. How can you make your team feel more accepted?

Notes

1 John Mackey and Raj Sisodia, *Conscious Capitalism: Liberating the Heroic Spirit of Business* (Boston: Harvard Business School Publishing Corporation, 2014), 226.

2 Ibid.

3 Ibid.

4 Ibid.

CHAPTER 9

Training Propagates Tenderness

"Do not primarily train men to work.
Train them to serve willingly and intelligently."

—J. C. Penney

When Lot was taken captive in the battle between the kings in the account in Genesis 14, his uncle Abram came to his rescue. "When Abram heard that his kinsman had been taken captive, he led forth his trained men, born in his house, 318 of them, and went in pursuit as far as Dan. And he divided his forces against them by night, he and his servants, and defeated them and pursued them to Hobah, north of Damascus. Then he brought back all the possessions, and also brought back his kinsman Lot with his possessions, and the women and the people" (Genesis 14:14-16).

Abram was successful in his rescue no doubt because God was with him and because he had a good strategy. Another reason Abram was successful is because of one word in the passage: *trained*. Abram had taken the time to train his men in advance, so that they would be ready for just such an occasion.

Good results in the business world don't just happen; they happen because people are prepared to make those results happen. Victor Lipman writes at Forbes.com that training and developing your people is an important business investment. *"Development planning doesn't have to be elaborate or costly.* At its core it's mostly a matter of good managers *taking the person-to-person time to understand their employees...* recognizing their skills and needs... and guiding them to fill in the gaps. If it's done well, the payoff can be substantial in terms of long-term loyalty. If it's not, the costs can be substantial in terms of long-term talent."[1]

Training is an area that often can be overlooked in making your business more profitable. Business owners may often think that they do not have time to devote to training their people, but training is a strategic component of growing your business. If you want to make your business scalable, then it is essential to make training part of your business culture.

Training doesn't just help your employees understand how to do the job better. It shows that you want to invest in your team. In Chapter 2, one survey respondent wished the boss knew "How training works." That's why the Culture Health Question for this chapter is: *Do employees believe leadership takes an active and ongoing interest in their professional and personal development?*

Investing time in training will provide you with long-term dividends in terms of how well you understand your business, how much your employees feel appreciated, and how ingrained your company culture becomes. But if you don't train your people, it will come back to bite you.

Here are three reasons why you should carve out time to train your team.

1. Training makes you understand your business better.
Developing training material causes you to think deeply about what you want your company to look like. For you to train your team, you first have to understand what it is you want to tell them (Luke 6:40). The teacher always learns more than the student. This is not to say that you have to create the training program yourself. But you do need to develop the goals for the training program. As Stephen R. Covey famously said in *The 7 Habits of Highly Effective People*, "Begin with the end in mind."[2]

As a result of the strategic plans you have created, your team must be prepared for the roles they will need to fill as the company changes. Think through what you want your company to look like down the road and create a training regimen that will get you there.

- To plan for the growth you will have, think through how your team's processes will have to change when you grow. Then teach your employees what they will need to know in the future so they will be prepared for the company's growth.

- Ask your team what challenges they face on the job, and you will discover the areas that you need to explain more fully. They will know firsthand the challenges of what the job requires better than you do.

- Survey your team for how they think their job could be done better. Then you can implement their process improvement suggestions as part of the training regimen.

2. Training shows you care about your team.
No one wants to do a job that they can't be good at. Taking the time to train your team shows that you care enough about them to help them be good at what they do and what you want them to become in the future. Your team will become in the future what you prepare them to do now. Explain to them how the training will help them.

They must see why it is important, how it will benefit them, and what will be the results.

> *Spend less time working in your business and more time working on your business.*

- Tell them why the company will benefit from the training they will receive. Explain why the time away from their day-to-day job will be worth it. Help them see how the objectives of the training meet the overall objectives of the company and the specific objectives of the work they do.

- Explain to them why the training program will be beneficial to them personally. Show how the training will help them become more competent and skilled in their field. Give them an understanding of how they will become more marketable in their profession as a result of mastering the training content.

- Help them to see how they will become more proficient in serving customers and/or their colleagues as a result of the training. Give them insight into how the company will grow and change because of their newly gained proficiency. Explain to them that this training will help them become more a part of the future of the company because the company's direction necessitates mastery of this material.

3. Training creates culture.
By training your team, you create an institutional knowledge that will be shared by everyone. That institutional knowledge over time will serve to form the culture of your company. The training will serve as a glue to connect everyone in a common experience that will produce common knowledge among the entire team.

Culture-shaping training must be mandatory. Everyone must go through the same training for the institutional culture to take hold. As a result of this training, everyone will know what you would do in certain situations, and they will know what you would not do in certain situations.

Although training takes time on the front end, it saves you time down the road by contributing to your company culture. And when you create the right culture, you don't even need to be physically present, because you will have trained your team to operate as if you were there.

Taking the time to invest in training will pay you dividends. You will be freed up to spend less time working *in* your business and more time working *on* your business. And it all starts by empowering employees to become the professionals that they *want* to be so they can become who you *need* them to be.

Reflection Questions

1. How do you need to prepare your employees to grow in the future?

2. What kind of training do your employees need? Do they fully understand the reasons for it?

3. What kind of institutional culture do you want to train your people to buy into?

Notes

1 Victor Lipman, "Why Employee Development Is Important, Neglected And Can Cost You Talent," *Forbes*, January 29, 2013; accessed at https://www.forbes.com/sites/victorlipman/2013/01/29/why-development-planning-is-important-neglected-and-can-cost-you-young-talent/#6cc5bb176f63. Emphasis original.

2 Stephen R. Covey, *The 7 Habits of Highly Effective People: Powerful Lessons in Personal Change* (New York: Fireside, 1990), 99.

CHAPTER 10

Flexibility Preserves Tenderness

"Competitiveness demands flexibility."

—David Cameron

In the Gospel of Matthew, Jesus and the disciples were walking through a planted field on the Sabbath. Since they were hungry, they plucked some of the grain and began to eat it. The Pharisees saw what they were doing and said that they were violating the commandment to rest on the Sabbath day. Jesus then rebuked them for their narrowmindedness and told them, "The Sabbath was made for man, not man for the Sabbath" (Mark 2:23-28).

Have you ever worked with a bean counter? Someone who feels that everything must comply with a set standard, just for the sake of standardization? While their zeal for the standard can be admirable, it is misplaced. They forget in their zeal why the standard exists. They forget that the standard was made for the employees, not the employees for the standard.

To create a Culture of Tenderness, flexibility must be valued in the workplace. In Chapter 2, a survey respondent expressed concern about the need to change how they do things: "Some conditions employees are dealing with which [sic] are legal but if adjusted would make for a much more positive attitude among employees." That's why this chapter's Culture Health Question is: *Does the workplace allow for flexibility to deal with the demands of the situation?*

Here are three perspectives to remember when incorporating flexibility into your workplace culture.

> *Humble leaders are not weak; they know who they are so they do not need to pretend to be someone they're not.*

1. Don't cling to rules.

Just like the Pharisees in Jesus's day, there are people in our workplaces who think that they are serving the organization by being dogmatic about rules (Mark 2:24). They feel that they are providing an essential function by enforcing the standard. But more often than not, this is not helpful.

Don't get me wrong. There are times when the standard is extremely important. The standard must be observed when veering from the standard involves doing illegal, unethical, or immoral behavior. The standard should never be violated in those cases.

Most of the time, however, the standard is simply a guideline, and overzealous adherence is a liability. Jim Collins in *Good to Great* explained that "the purpose of bureaucracy is to compensate for incompetence and lack of discipline."[1] If your workplace relies heavily on bureaucracy, then you may have too many incompetent people at your company who are not able to discipline themselves from within. At the same time, it is possible that you personally may have a managerial perspective that relies too heavily on control.

2. Exhibit humility.

Humility is a key virtue in cultivating flexibility. Being humble takes the focus off yourself and puts it on the needs of others. Self-centered people lack humility and express a sense of self-importance. They are more likely to defend their ideas and not be flexible. They feel like they need to have it their way just because they want it done their way. But when people are truly humble, they are more able to adjust to the situation and meet the needs of others. Kenman Wong and Scott Rae explain in *Business for the Common Good* that "leaders that exhibit genuine humility find that they are less rigid in their categories, more open to learning from a variety of sources, including employees and other subordinates, and thus model this kind of openness to new information."[2]

Jim Collins discerned the same truth when he described the Level 5 leader in *Good to Great* as an executive who possessed personal humility yet professional will.[3] Humble leaders are therefore not weak; they know who they are so they do not need to pretend to be someone they're not.

By exhibiting humility, you will show that you do not have to prove yourself to be someone—because you already are someone in the eyes of God (James 4:10). The people you work with will feel that they can drop their guards around you because they won't feel like they have to prove themselves either.

As an Active Leader, you will be well served to get yourself out of the way in order to lead your organization. After all, it's not about you. It's about doing what needs to be done to bring out the best in your team, so collectively, you can serve your customer the best that you can.

3. Be willing to change.

Former British Prime Minister David Cameron wisely said, "Competitiveness demands flexibility." If you are going to be competitive as a company, it will be evidenced in how open you are as a leader to change. If you are not open to change, then the people who work for you will not be open to it either.

The Pharisees were not willing to change to Jesus's way of thinking. Jesus wanted them to abandon their man-made rules that interpreted the Scripture and instead embrace the living God who stood right in front of them.

You, as a leader, set the tone for your organization. You must reject rigid adherence to rules and instead embrace a personal humility to create a culture where people will be willing to change. The people who work for you must know that they will not be slapped down if they try to do something new.

Max De Pree, the former CEO of Herman Miller, defined leadership in *Leadership Is an Art* as "liberating people to do what is required of them in the most effective and humane way possible."[4] You have an opportunity to unleash the creative potential in everyone on your team. However, they must be purposely cultivated for change so that they can have the flexibility to deal with the demands of the situation.

To create a flexible work environment, *you* need to be flexible. Your team must see evidenced in you a willingness to abandon rules that don't serve the company anymore. They must see a personal humility demonstrated in your actions daily. And they must see an openness to embrace new ways of doing things that you might not have tried before. If you can live that attitude of flexibility, then you will be able to inculcate that attitude in your team.

Reflection Questions

1. Before you begin this process of change for your people, what is your comfort level toward change?

2. Do you feel secure enough in who you are to handle a constantly changing work environment?

3. How do you need to prepare yourself to comfort, inspire, and lead your people through the process of change?

Notes

1 Jim Collins, *Good to Great: Why Some Companies Make the Leap ... and Others Don't* (New York: Harper Collins, 2001), 121.

2 Kenman L. Wong and Scott B. Rae, *Business for the Common Good: A Christian Vision for the Marketplace* (Madison, WI: InterVarsity Press, 2011), 201.

3 Jim Collins, *Good to Great: Why Some Companies Make the Leap ... and Others Don't* (New York: Harper Collins, 2001), 20.

4 Max De Pree, *Leadership Is an Art* (New York: Doubleday, 2004), xxii.

CHAPTER 11

Praise Professes Tenderness

"The sweetest of all sounds is praise."

—Xenophon

Nearly 20 years ago, I worked for a boss who was effusive in his praise. Paul had a policy of always praising employees publicly. Whenever I did something well, he was quick to tell me and everyone else in the office about what I had done.

As the new head of media relations, I organized a press conference about one of the new initiatives, but I did not realize at the time that the organization had never before held a successful press conference. I worked on developing the pitch for each angle, identified every reporter who would care, and followed up to make sure someone from each news outlet was coming. As a result, when the appointed time of the press conference arrived, Paul walked into a packed room with six or seven television cameras pointing at him. He was so overjoyed that I can still remember his enthusiasm today.

Have you ever worked for someone who affirmed you? Someone who sincerely praised you when you did well? If you have, then you will no doubt never forget that experience. Nearly 20 years later, I still remember Paul's reaction.

Everyone wants to hear that someone else appreciates them. But how often do you go out of your way to express appreciation to others? Work would be a better place if you fostered a Culture of Tenderness at your workplace. In Chapter 2, a survey respondent said, "HOW IMPORTANT IT IS TO TELL PEOPLE THAT THEY ARE DOING A GOOD JOB, INSTEAD OF ONLY COMPLAINING." That's why this chapter's Culture Health Question is: *Does leadership regularly give praise for what employees do well?*

You might think it will sound forced or cheesy if you say that you appreciate someone else, but you probably just feel awkward saying it. If someone else has genuinely praised you, then you know how good that feels when someone says that to you. Since you want to hear it, learn how to overcome that awkwardness and become intentional as an Active Leader about expressing appreciation to the people at your workplace. Creating a Culture of Tenderness starts with having the right perspective and being willing to verbalize your appreciation.

Here are three guidelines for giving compliments.

1. Be genuine.
Praise should be for building up people, not for using them (Romans 12:9). Before you give someone a compliment, check your motives. Why do you want to give this person a compliment? Do you mean what you are thinking? Or are you trying to manipulate them?

Make sure that you do not have any ulterior motives. Don't tell them they did a good job right before you ask them to do something difficult. I once had a boss who would praise me only when he wanted something from me. He seemed to use the compliment as leverage to get me to do something that I didn't think we should do. As much as I wanted to believe that he was sincere in his compliment, I felt manipulated by the timing of his requests.

Give compliments to build a relationship with your people. Show them by your words that you value what they do. They may not get any encouraging words from anyone else in their lives, so you can have a powerful influence in their lives if you speak life into them.

I don't give these guidelines for you to overthink giving compliments. Just express what you naturally feel. If you really mean the compliment, then you should be willing to say it—because if you truly believe it, then they will want to hear it.

2. Refrain from sarcasm.

Sarcasm is a guaranteed way to destroy any goodwill you can generate by giving praise to your team. People tend to use sarcasm because they feel uncomfortable saying genuine affirmations; however, sarcasm will negate the effect of the compliment you are trying to give because it will be misunderstood.

People rarely hear genuine affirmations, so they don't know how to handle compliments. If you are sarcastic about the compliment, then they will think that you really didn't mean it because they will not know if you mean what you say or if you are just joking (Proverbs 26:18-19). Sarcastic joking will not help create a Culture of Tenderness.

If you really mean the compliment, then you should be willing to say it—because if you truly believe it, then they will want to hear it.

Your team needs to know that you mean the compliments, so say what you mean and mean what you say.

Most likely the people who work for you are not used to compliments that are heartfelt and genuine. If you give compliments without sarcasm or irony, they will stand out. If you look your team in the eye and give them a genuine compliment, it will have a profound impact on them. In fact, it may have more of an impact than you may realize.

3. Repeat yourself—again and again.

You cannot say compliments just once. You will have to do it over and over and over. I once heard a (fictional) story about a young man who married a young woman. On their wedding day, the man told his wife that he loved her. For the next 50 years he never said those words to her again. Exasperated after 50 years without hearing her husband say, "I love you," the wife approached her husband. "Why have you never told me you loved me these 50 years?" Looking up from his newspaper, he said, "I told you I loved you when I married you, and I'll let you know if I ever change my mind."

Unlike the man in the story, you will need to say compliments regularly—particularly because people are not used to hearing positive things said to them by other people. If you have not been in the habit of complimenting your people on a regular basis, then they will not believe you said it the first time, or the second, or the third. They will have to hear it again and again and again before they believe that you mean it.

Be sure to compliment in private and in public. If they hear you say it just to them, they may not think that you mean it. They will know you mean it if you will say it in public settings in front of their colleagues as well.

When you first start giving your people genuine affirmations, it might be difficult to look them in the eyes and say it without sarcasm. Don't give up (2 Thessalonians 3:13; Galatians 6:9). Though it may feel awkward at first, it will get easier with time. After you have done it for a while, it will become a way of life, and it will yield results far beyond your expectations.

Reflection Questions

1. Have you ever worked for someone who affirmed you— someone who sincerely praised you when you did well?

2. Why do you give people compliments? Do you mean what you are thinking? Or are you trying to manipulate them?

3. How often do you go out of your way to express genuine appreciation to others?

CHAPTER 12

Feedback Provides Tenderness

"We all need people who will give us feedback.
That's how we improve."

—Bill Gates

In my first managerial role, I had a difficult time providing constructive feedback to my assistant because I was so nervous about saying anything I perceived was negative. I did not like the idea of conflict, so I tried to avoid it as much as possible. When it came time to critique her performance in her first annual review, I could barely get the words out. As much as she needed the feedback, I had a hard time being able to voice anything critical.

Over the next months, I learned how to become more open in my critiques. I was able to tell her what she needed to do to become better at her job and to become more helpful to me. She became extremely proficient at her work. In fact, when I left the organization to move into a vice president role, she became my successor.

In my new supervisory role as a vice president, I was much more comfortable and confident giving personnel reviews to my assistant and the others on my staff. I realized how important it was for me to get over any issues I had with giving criticism so that I could help my team grow in their responsibilities. I understood that to be unclear is to be unkind.

I have valued constructive feedback from my bosses, and I am sure that you have valued the insight and input your bosses have provided you. Since you are in a leadership role, your team will need constructive feedback from you to produce consistent improvement. You will help your team stay on track if you provide them with those compassionate and positive course corrections.

In Chapter 2, a survey respondent said, "That I need more realtime [sic] feedback." In response, our Culture Health Question this chapter is: *Does leadership compassionately give constructive feedback to help employees improve?*

When you correct your team, what you say matters as much as how you say it. Instead of pointing out only what your team is doing wrong, give them constructive feedback in a way that they don't feel inadequate because of what they are doing wrong. As the adage goes, you catch more flies with honey than with vinegar.

Your Culture of Tenderness will depend on the tone you set as an Active Leader. If you see yourself more as a coach instead of a boss or a manager, then the input you give them will have a more powerful and positive impact. Here are three pointers for giving your team constructive feedback for their consistent improvement.

1. Reverse the roles.
Before you give feedback to your team members, think through what it would feel like if the roles were reversed. Remember the Golden Rule (Matthew 7:12). When you were the one being corrected, how did you want to be spoken to? What words would have made a positive impact on you? How could your bosses have used your

performance reviews to motivate you better? Prepare to give your feedback with the answers to those questions in mind.

Think of the best boss you ever had. Why did they impact you so much? What did they say that made them so memorable? What could you say that would make you as memorable? On the other hand, your bosses may have been stern and harsh with you. They may have cut you down in performance reviews. That does not mean that you need to replicate that

To be unclear is to be unkind.

behavior with your own team. Inflicting your team with the same invective that you received is not a healthy way to approach working with your team. Decide that you will be the one to break that cycle. The words you use can build up or tear down (Proverbs 18:21). Choose to say words that will change lives for the better.

2. Celebrate forward progress.
Your team will not be perfect at what they do initially. Even with training, it will take them time until they are competent at what they were hired to do. Celebrating even the little steps forward will show that you appreciate the effort they are putting in.

If you consistently reiterate your belief that they will be able to perform at the desired level, they will rise to the challenge. Because you are celebrating their forward progress, they will want to prove you right. They may rely on your belief that they can perform at the desired level. Because of your investment in them, eventually they will believe that they can do it too.

When you were in their situation—if you ever were—think through the input that would have been meaningful to you. At what points in your career do you wish someone had encouraged you? What words would have been helpful for you to hear at those points in your career? How do you wish someone would have built you up in those situations?

By providing constructive feedback they need to hear, you will help them improve. Because you are consistently celebrating their forward progress, you will make them want to improve.

3. Affirm everyone's intrinsic dignity.

Keep your interactions positive with everyone on the team. Make sure that they know that you appreciate them and value their contributions. Tell them how much you believe in their ability to do the work necessary. At the same time, you don't have to overlook nonperformers. You are not doing anyone any favors if you condone poor performance.

Because every person on your team is made in the image of God, they have an intrinsic dignity. Kenman Wong and Scott Rae reinforce this idea in *Business for the Common Good*: "Keeping staff when they are not doing their work properly, when they are a poor fit for the position or there is not enough work to justify their employment, does not serve to enhance their dignity."[1] If they are not a good fit at your workplace, then God has another place for them to serve. If you keep them at your workplace, then you are holding them back from what God made them to do. You can still affirm someone's dignity and decide they need to go work somewhere else.

If you have the right team, then you will want to keep them, and reiterating your belief in them will help you retain your team. If you have the right people on board, then creating a Culture of Tenderness will encourage them to work harder. If you consistently give them positive and constructive feedback, they will want to stay and work even harder for you. Deciding to view your role more as a coach instead of a boss will help your team gain the skills and the confidence to perform at a higher level. As a result, they will enjoy their roles more—and you will too.

Reflection Questions

1. How would you want to be spoken to if you were the one being corrected?

2. What words could you use to make a positive impact on your team?

3. How could you do a better job (than your former bosses) in giving constructive feedback?

Notes

1 Kenman L. Wong and Scott B. Rae, *Business for the Common Good: A Christian Vision for the Marketplace* (Madison, WI: InterVarsity Press, 2011), 205.

CHAPTER 13

Team

*"Teamwork is the ability to work
together toward a common vision.
The ability to direct individual accomplishments
toward organizational objectives."*

—Andrew Carnegie

One of my bosses, Phil, played professional football for eight years. He told me there were a lot of guys in the National Football League who had more raw talent than he did. Phil said he played as long as he did in the NFL because he worked harder than they did.

Even though Phil may not have had the raw talent that other players on the team did, he was willing to do what was necessary for the team. Unfortunately, Phil's example does not seem to happen that often in today's workplace, but understandably so. John Mackey and Raj Sisodia remind us in *Conscious Capitalism* that "many people hate their work and are stressed out by their jobs. The workplace is frequently a pressure-cooker environment, working conditions are often poor, team members are not valued as human beings, and colleagues view one another as competitors and threats."[1]

Due to this scenario in the American workplace, it should be no surprise that employees do not believe the companies they work for have a positive morale. Gallup's 2017 *State of the American Workplace* report found that employees do not believe much in the leadership of the companies where they work. Only 15 percent strongly agreed that their company's leadership inspires them to be "enthusiastic about the future."[2]

> *Active Leaders are all about their team.*

There is good news, however. Gallup says companies can increase this percentage if their leadership will focus more on their employees.[3] Kenman Wong and Scott Rae agree in *Business for the Common Good* that team members can be inspired when their leaders believe that "the people who report to [them] are made in God's image and thus have intrinsic dignity, not simply replaceable cogs in a company's machinery. Regardless of their competence, they have the right to be treated with respect and are not to be demeaned by their leaders."[4]

Active Leaders are all about their team. They epitomize Jesus' teachings: Whoever would be the greatest must first be a servant (Matthew 23:11). Active Leaders recognize the influence they have, and they intentionally use every opportunity to wield that influence to benefit their followers. Active Leaders are similar to Jim Collins' Level 5 leaders, who possess personal humility yet evidence professional will. As Collins says in *Good to Great*, "Level 5 leaders channel their ego needs away from themselves and into the larger goal of building a great company. It's not that Level 5 leaders have no ego or self-interest. Indeed, they are incredibly ambitious—*but their ambition is first and foremost for the institution, not themselves.*"[5]

In this section, we will explore what a Team environment can look like. Over the next five chapters, we will discuss the following five topics.

Vision Fuels a Team
Leadership must ensure that everyone understands and identifies with the vision of the organization. Leaders must continually cast vision to help everyone be on the same page about where the organization is headed.

Values Focus a Team
Leadership must ensure that everyone subscribes to the organization's core values. Leaders must inform team members of the organization's values when they are hired and must continually remind the team of the organization's values.

Purpose Fulfills a Team
Leadership must explain the importance of the work that the organization does to the extent that team members believe the work they do matters. If leaders don't believe the work matters, then neither will the team.

Performance Fashions a Team
Leadership must convey to the team that everyone's individual performance is important to moving the organization forward. Everyone—team leaders and team members alike—must believe that doing their best at their job is important to the company's success.

Colleagues Form a Team
Leadership must ensure that everyone feels that their colleagues are all pulling their own weight. If anyone thinks that others aren't doing their part, it will erode everyone's desire to work as hard as they could.

I hope the following chapters will serve as a springboard for you to see how you can serve your team through your Active Leadership. By intentionally leading through serving, I believe you will enhance your employees' perspective of how they can become the people they want to be by working as a team in your company.

Reflection Questions

1. How much does your company work as a team?

2. How focused have you been up to this point on having your team think like a team?

3. What can you do to help your team act more like a team in the future?

Notes

1 John Mackey and Raj Sisodia, *Conscious Capitalism: Liberating the Heroic Spirit of Business* (Harvard Business School Publishing Corporation, Boston, 2014), 85.

2 Gallup, Inc., *State of the American Workplace* (Washington, D.C.: Gallup, 2017); accessed at http://www.gallup.com/reports/199961/state-american-workplace-report-2017.aspx.

3 Ibid.

4 Kenman L. Wong and Scott B. Rae, *Business for the Common Good: A Christian Vision for the Marketplace* (Madison, WI: InterVarsity Press, 2011), 202.

5 Jim Collins, *Good to Great: Why Some Companies Make the Leap ... and Others Don't* (New York: Harper Collins, 2001), 21. Emphasis original.

CHAPTER 14

Vision Fuels a Team

"Leadership is the capacity to translate vision into reality."
—Warren Bennis

When Blake Mycoskie traveled to Argentina for a vacation in 2006, he did not realize that trip would change his life forever—and the lives of more than a million others too. While in Argentina, Mycoskie made two discoveries: the *alpargata* shoe—a comfortable shoe worn by native Argentines—and the ubiquity of poor, shoeless children. Being an American serial entrepreneur, Mycoskie connected the two: What if he could sell modified *alpargata* shoes to Americans, and then give a pair of shoes to a child in need for every pair sold?

When Mycoskie came back to the US, he brought back three duffle bags full of 250 sample *alpargata* shoes—and a vision of both selling and giving away 10,000 pairs of shoes.[1] That vision created a business model for TOMS that attracted a dedicated and loyal team of people who believed in the same vision that Mycoskie did. They loved what TOMS represented, and they wanted to be part of the story that was unfolding.

You can attract the same kind of team if you have a vision worth sharing. To create a Team Culture, you must have a vision that everyone at your workplace can identify with. In Chapter 3, one of the survey respondents said he wanted the boss to know "How to motivate employees." As a result, this chapter's Culture Health Question is: *Does everyone understand and identify with the vision of the organization?*

1. The Definition of Vision

To explain what I mean by vision, I will provide my definition: *A vision is a picture of a future state taken from a present vantage point.* Let's break down the components of the definition.

Working toward a grand vision will excite your people by the prospect of doing work that holds more meaning to them.

Picture

As implied by the word "picture," a vision is a visual image. It can be bleary or it can be in focus, depending on how clear it is in the minds of the ones envisioning it. Over time, the image of the vision can become more in focus as the ones with the vision fine-tune what they see.

Future State

A vision is set in the future. The clarity of the image in the minds of the ones envisioning it has nothing to do with how far into the future the vision is set. Instead, it has everything to do with how clearly they can imagine what that future state would look like.

Present Vantage Point

A vision has just as much to do with the present as it does with the future. The greater the difference between the present state and the future state—i.e., how much needs to change between Point A and Point B—can make the vision more desirable to achieve.

2. The Importance of Vision

Would you ever start driving on your vacation and not know where you were going to end up? Of course not. However, this is exactly what happens with most companies. They don't have a clear destination, so they can get off track easily because they don't really know what it looks like to be on track.

Most companies have not done the soul searching to know why they are in business to begin with. If they don't know why they are in business, then they can't communicate it to their employees or customers. Simon Sinek explains how companies can encourage more loyalty in *Start with Why*:

> [M]ost companies have no clue why their customers are their customers. ... If companies don't know why their customers are their customers, odds are good that they don't know why their employees are their employees either.
>
> If most companies don't really know why their customers are their customers or why their employees are their employees, then how do they know how to attract more employees and encourage loyalty among those they already have? ...
>
> There are only two ways to influence human behavior: you can manipulate it or you can inspire it.[2]

You can provide the inspiration your employees are looking for with a clear, compelling vision of where you are going. Without a vision, you may end up resorting to manipulating your team to get them to do what you want. However, a more effective and more powerful way to influence your team is to inspire them with a vision.

3. The Power of Vision

People at your workplace want to be inspired by doing work that makes a difference, and they want to work towards creating a world that resonates with their personal passions. A clear and compelling vision is like a three-pronged electrical plug that you would plug into a receptacle. The first prong draws to you the very people who want to be part of achieving the vision. The second repels from you the people who will not want to help you achieve the vision. The third grounds your team when their results are discouraging.

To have a compelling vision, it's important to clearly identify where you want your company to go (Habakkuk 2:2). Doing this kind of company soul-searching will help you create a powerful tool in pruning and invigorating your workforce. Working toward a grand vision will excite your people by the prospect of doing work that holds more meaning to them. And you will do a favor to those who don't want to be a part of accomplishing the vision by encouraging them to find some other place to work. That way, those motivated by the vision will feel doubly blessed. They will enjoy the journey toward accomplishing the vision—without those who don't want to go there.

Reflection Questions

1. Up to this point, how clearly have you been able to see a vision for your company?

2. What vision for your company would most inspire your team?

3. What vision would most help define your company?

Notes

1 Blake Mycoskie, *Start Something That Matters* (New York: Spiegel & Grau, 2011), 3-19.

2 Simon Sinek, *Start with Why: How Great Leaders Inspire Everyone to Take Action* (New York: Penguin Group, 2009), 16-17.

CHAPTER 15

Values Focus a Team

*"When your values are clear to you,
making decisions becomes easier."*

—Roy E. Disney

Daniel Henderson tells a story about the importance of values in the workplace.

> [A] few years ago I was called as a senior pastor of a church in deep trouble. ... In the process of seeking to shepherd the church to health and guide the staff, I conducted an experiment a few months after my arrival. For years, the church had emphasized fifteen guiding principles that uniquely identified their congregation and clarified their ministry strategy. So, at an all-staff gathering, I handed out blank sheets of paper and asked the staff to list these fifteen values. ... After collecting the papers, I discovered that one staff member listed five, most could recall one or two, and some had no idea what I was talking about. It mattered little if the church had five or fifteen key values. What did matter is whether the leaders understood and "owned" them as essential and relevant to the ministry.[1]

Just as in Daniel Henderson's church, your workplace should be able to identify the values that will guide *how* you do *what* you do in order to have a Team Culture. While it doesn't matter whether you have five or fifteen values (although I will say it is easier to memorize five instead of fifteen), it matters that your team understands and owns your workplace values.

If the company leadership is not intentional about identifying or living their values, other unintentional values will fill the void. In Chapter 3, one survey respondent wished the boss knew "The negative effect her management has on morale and quality." Accordingly, this chapter's Culture Health Question is: *Does everyone subscribe to the organization's values?*

Institutionalized values are important to your organization because they serve to form the culture of your workplace. Your organization's values will provide boundaries and guidance for individual and company-wide behavior.

Company-wide values will provide the reasoning behind your company practices and serve as the standards to clarify organizational policies and procedures. Your company values will therefore make the work that you do more meaningful. These standards will help to draw the right people to you, and they will also serve to repel the wrong people from you.

Instituting your values can be a lengthy process. To implement your values into your workplace, follow these three steps.

1. Isolate your core values.

The first thing involved in instituting your values is knowing what values you want to uphold. Determining your core values is essentially figuring out *how* you do *what* you do. It may take some time to understand what is really important to you as a leader and to your team. Isolating your company values should not be treated flippantly.

It should take place as part of regular strategic planning process or perhaps at an annual company leadership retreat.

Once you have identified what attributes you want to have exemplified by your team, encapsulate in a word or phrase each attribute you want inculcated in your work environment. Develop a list of the words or phrases, and give each a short definition or explanation.

Your workplace culture will be created by how well you live your values.

Don't use words you don't mean. If "excellence" doesn't describe how you will do your work, then don't use it as a value. If "honesty" doesn't describe how you will conduct your business, then don't use it as a value.

You probably don't want to have as many as fifteen values. They are not helpful if they cannot be memorized, as Daniel Henderson's story demonstrated. When values are internalized, they will help clarify your culture.

2. Explain your core values.
Once you have isolated your core values, then explain to your employees what they are. Even if your employees were involved in the process of developing your values, it's always important to remind them what your values mean.

Be clear about your expectations with your team. Tell them why you came up with this list of values and what each word or phrase means, and explain to them what each value looks like in action. Only that way will they know how to replicate those values as they do their work.

It's helpful to post your values prominently so everyone can reference them. Even if the values may seem like common sense, it is important that everyone be reminded what they are. It will take some time for everyone—even you—to get used to the stated expectations.

3. Live your core values.

More important than isolating or explaining your core values is living them out daily. Even if you isolate your core values and explain them, they will mean nothing to anyone on your team if you, as a leader, do not live by them. By intentionally living your stated core values day after day, they will become part of your culture over time because your team will see you demonstrating them in front of their eyes. As an Active Leader, you need to be both the poster child and the enforcer for your company values. You cannot delegate this responsibility to your human resources department. This is your responsibility as a leader.

Daniel Henderson explains that values are powerful when they are both "declared" and "demonstrated." However, he says the opposite effect happens if they are only just declared. Here is an "equation" he uses to make his point.

Declared + Demonstrated = Integrity
Declared − Demonstrated = Hypocrisy[2]

Scripture reinforces this point: "Whoever walks in integrity walks securely" (Proverbs 10:9). If you violate your own values, then it will be worse than if you had never declared them. Your workplace culture will be created by how well you live your values. What you say matters, but how you systematize the culture will make the difference.

It's the 1,000 little things you do over time that creates and reinforces that cultural mindset. If you are intentional and consistent, you can design and implement a process to institute your values and create the kind of culture you want to see in your workplace.

Reflection Questions

1. What are ways that you always behave or operate? What are ways that you never do?

2. What do you want the workplace to feel like? What do you want to define the company?

3. What behaviors do you want to have in place, even if you are personally not present?

Notes

1 Daniel Henderson, *The Deeper Life: Satisfying the 8 Vital Longings of the Soul* (Bloomington, MN: Bethany House Publishers, 2014), 79.

2 Ibid., 82.

CHAPTER 16

Purpose Fulfills a Team

"Choose a job you love, and you will never have to work a day in your life."

—Confucius

In the science fiction action film *The Terminator*, humankind has produced cyborg machines that have become self-aware and taken over the world, bringing on a nuclear apocalypse. The remaining humans are led by John Connor to band together and form the Resistance. The movie is about how one of the cyborgs goes back in time to kill Sarah Connor—the mother of the Resistance leader—and about how one of the humans, Kyle Reese, goes back in time to save her.

Kyle has heard the stories from John about the legendary Sarah Connor: how heroic she was, and how she prepared John for his destiny. When Kyle finally meets Sarah, he finds her to be a fraidy cat, and she doesn't feel up to the task Kyle is calling her to. In fact, she thinks he must be looking for the wrong person. However, after becoming aware of what will happen in the future, she is changed.

The once fraidy cat resolves to become the survivalist she has to be because she has come to understand her purpose.[1]

Before Sarah met Kyle, she saw no need to move from the city to the country, to learn how to fight, or to prepare to survive a nuclear war. But upon learning what was destined to happen, she was inspired to embrace a new purpose for her life, and she was willing to learn and do whatever it took to prepare her future son to become the leader of the Resistance. At that point, she realized that the work she did really mattered.

At your company, you can prepare your employees to have passion for their work like Sarah Connor had for hers (although perhaps not as intense as hers). You can help your team to cultivate what the Scripture describes as "singleness of purpose" (1 Chronicles 12:33). By developing a purpose behind your company, you can help your team find true meaning in the work that they do.

In Chapter 3, one of the survey respondents wanted the boss to know "I hate my job." Along those lines, the Culture Health Question for this chapter is: *Does everyone believe the organization's work matters?*

Through your company, you can make a difference larger than your company. Your company can bring out the best in everyone on the team through your purpose.

1. The Importance of Purpose

Your purpose can be defined as *why* you do *what* you do. John Mackey and Raj Sisodia define purpose in *Conscious Capitalism* as "the difference you're trying to make in the world."[2]

> Purpose is something we can never take for granted; the moment we do, it starts to be forgotten and soon disappears. It has to be at the forefront of consciousness (and therefore decision making) literally all the time. When the purpose is clear, leadership teams can make quicker

and better decisions. Clarity of purpose also leads to bolder decisions. Rather than adjusting decisions according to the winds of public opinion or changes in the competitive environment, decisions in a purpose-driven company take those things into consideration while also being informed by something more soulful and sturdy. This leads to superior overall performance. Purpose-informed decision making is a critical connection point between clarity of purpose and superior performance, financially and otherwise.[3]

Note that the purpose of your company is different than making money. Do not expect your team to work solely for a paycheck. Inspire them to something more. While money provides options, it does not provide happiness. Helen Keller said, "Many persons have the wrong idea of what constitutes true happiness. It is not obtained through self-gratification but through fidelity to a worthy purpose."

2. The Benefits of Purpose

By working to fulfill your company purpose, your customers will take notice. They will feel good about their interactions with your company because your company's higher purpose will show through. That experience will enhance your brand and develop deeper customer trust. Because your customers will feel increased value from their business with you, you will retain more customers and possibly be able to charge more for your product or service. Therefore, you will make more money in the process.

Your company's purpose cannot be created and ignored. It must become the core of the company.

Through working toward a higher purpose, you will foster greater employee engagement. Your employees will sense they are doing meaningful work and their contributions are important. Your team will feel more enthusiastic about coming to work because they will be doing something more than just making money. That enthusiasm will attract a customer base who is enthusiastic about the same purpose.

Because of the way your company purpose resonates with your customer base, you will have more influence with your community where you live and work because the good you do through your company purpose will enhance your brand.

3. The Search for Purpose

If your company has lost its purpose, you may have to go back to your roots and rediscover why it was founded. If you have never before articulated your company's purpose, you may want to embark on what John Mackey and Raj Sisodia call a "purpose search."

> The process includes representatives of all the stakeholder groups: the senior leadership of the company and some board members, team members, customers, investors, suppliers, and members of the community. All have a stake in the flourishing of the business, and all have a vision of what the purpose of that enterprise could be. When we bring these major stakeholders together to discover or create a higher purpose, some amazing things can happen. The exchange of information, values, and unique perspectives about the business can result in the rediscovery or creation of the company's higher purpose in a fairly short time— usually within a few days, and sometimes even in a single day if it is a really engaged process and is facilitated by a skilled consultant.[4]

Once you have developed your company's purpose, the real work begins. The company's purpose must be integrated into every facet, every communication, and every decision of the company. It must be displayed in the leaders' directions and the team's actions. Your company's purpose cannot be created and ignored. It must become the core of the company.

By articulating and intentionally working toward a higher purpose in your interactions with your employees and customers, your company will make a significant impact. You will be able to inspire your people, create a better workplace, strengthen your relationship with customers, and enhance your profitability. As a result, working toward a higher purpose will have a transformational effect on your employees, customers, and community—and on you.

Reflection Questions

1. Why does the work you do matter?

2. Other than making money, why is the work your company does meaningful to you personally?

3. What would make working for your company more meaningful to your team?

Notes

1 *The Terminator*, directed by James Cameron, MGM, 1984.

2 John Mackey and Raj Sisodia, *Conscious Capitalism: Liberating the Heroic Spirit of Business* (Boston: Harvard Business School Publishing Corporation, 2014), 47.

3 Ibid., 49.

4 Ibid., 65-66.

CHAPTER 17

Performance Fashions a Team

"I can only control my own performance."

—Michael Phelps

James Madison University football head coach Mike Houston was a man on a mission. When hired to lead the program in January 2016, he planned to bring the Dukes to an FCS national championship. However, he didn't realize how quickly he would reach that goal.

The Dukes had seen a national title once before. In 2004, they went 9-2 in the regular season, 7-1 in their conference, and won their playoff games 14-13, 14-13, and 48-34, ending with a 31-21 national championship game. However, the Dukes had not racked up three appearances in the playoffs since 2008. In the 2015 season, the JMU Dukes had gone 9-2 overall in the regular season and 6-2 in their conference games, only to lose their first FCS playoff game 38-44.

All that changed when Mike Houston took the helm. In the first year of his leadership, the Dukes regained the glory they had achieved in 2004. They went 10-1 in the regular season, 8-0 in conference play, and then decisively won their playoff games 55-22, 65-7, and 27-17, culminating in a 28-14 win for the national championship.

When I asked Mike Houston about what goes into making a great team, he said, "As a leader you have to give your players an understanding that they are an important part of the process. Everyone has a role. Everyone has to embrace their role at their highest level."[1] When Mike Houston came to the JMU, not everyone was playing at his highest level. He created a Team Culture by emphasizing how valuable every member of the team was to the overall success of the team: Everyone had to be on board, and everyone had to believe that they had a part to play.

This team concept is similar to the picture of the body of Christ expressed in 1 Corinthians 12: "For just as the body is one and has many members, and all the members of the body, though many, are one body, so it is with Christ. … For the body does not consist of one member but of many" (1 Corinthians 12:12, 14). All the members of the body have to see themselves as part of the body. If they don't see how they fit as part of the body, then the body doesn't function as it should. In Chapter 3, one of the survey respondents wanted the boss to know "All of the tasks I'm capable of completing." Therefore, this chapter's Culture Health Question for your workplace is: *Does everyone believe their individual performance is necessary to move the organization forward?*

You can develop a team environment in your company by implementing the principles that Coach Houston put into practice with the JMU Dukes. To help you understand the performance mentality that is needed for your team to thrive, use these three concepts as a foundation.

1. Able

Everyone on your team needs to believe they are able to do their job, and they are able to make a difference for the team. All work has value. It is your job as a leader to make sure that everyone on your team sees that their work is valuable and valued. By letting them know that you value their work, they will take pride in what they do and they will do it with all their ability (Ecclesiastes 9:10; Colossians 3:23).

Every role in the company is as important to the success of the company as every other role. That means that you help the people in sales as well as those in accounting understand they are just as important to the overall success of the company as the other department is (1 Corinthians 12:22). When everyone realizes they need to do their part, then you will create the culture to sustain that kind of thinking.

> *Only when your team is internally strong can it be externally focused.*

If, however, a particular kind of work is demeaned as being less important, then those who do that work will feel defensive around others on the team. They may feel that they are not part of the team or—worse yet—that they want to retaliate against the team. Only when your team is internally strong can it be externally focused. When you show them that who they are is important to you and what they do is important to you, they will bring that same mindset to your customers.

2. Dependable

It is important to emphasize that everyone on the team can make a difference for the overall success of the team, and everyone on the team is dependent on everyone else on the team (1 Corinthians 12:20). If your team embraces that concept, it will help them understand that others are counting on them.

Everyone on the team needs to realize that they matter to the team, and what they do matters to the team as well (1 Corinthians 12:26). Unless everyone believes the role they play is important, they will not do it to the best of their ability. But if they can see that what they do fits into the big picture, they are more likely to give their all.

If the housekeeping staff of a hospital doesn't understand how important cleanliness is to the care of the patients, then the hospital could well be closed due to insanitary conditions. Since even mopping floors makes an important contribution to the success of the entire team, you can explain the importance behind every other kind of work as well. Everyone on the team should have a perspective that they will stand by their work because they understand that others depend on them to do good work.

3. Accountable

Because everyone is interdependent—dependent on everyone else—everyone on the team is accountable to everyone else on the team. Every department has a stake in every other department doing their best. Patrick Lencioni explains in *The Advantage* that "accountability is about having the courage to confront someone about their deficiencies and then to stand in the moment and deal with their reaction, which may not be pleasant. It is a selfless act, one rooted in a word that I don't use lightly in a business book: *love*. To hold someone accountable is to care about them enough to risk having them blame you for pointing out their deficiencies."[2]

That does not mean that one department should be allowed to accuse another department of not doing their job in order to deflect attention from their own deficiencies; however, it does mean that every department should have the same goal. You, as a leader, may have to speak with other leaders to address company issues, especially if there are problems between departments. You will have to care enough about the other leaders on the team to confront them one-on-one—for their benefit and for the benefit of the company.

Turf wars cannot be permitted because every department is on the same team. All information should be freely shared by each department. There can be no silos separating departments from each other. Secrecy and self-preserving attitudes will break down a team spirit and lead to suspicion and mistrust.

Every department is just as important, so they are equals. There should be a mutual respect and appreciation for the role that each department has. Every department should evidence a willingness to serve each other to achieve the overall company goals (Galatians 5:13).

By valuing individual performance in the context of team performance, everyone will see how important they are in big picture. By stressing how everyone on the team is dependent on everyone else on the team, it shows how much your team needs each other to be successful. And finally, by emphasizing the importance of accountability between departments, you will develop the openness necessary for true teamwork.

Reflection Questions

1. Does everyone on the team see how they are able to contribute to the success of the team?

2. Does everyone see how they need to be dependable and how others depend on them?

3. Does everyone understand that they must be accountable to everyone else on the team?

Notes

1 Coach Mike Houston, telephone interview, May 16, 2017.

2 Patrick Lencioni, *The Advantage: Why Organizational Health Trumps Everything Else in Business* (San Francisco: Jossey-Bass, 2012), 57. Emphasis original.

CHAPTER 18

Colleagues Form a Team

"We rarely celebrate individual goals.
Instead we celebrate team goals."

—Mike Houston

Could you imagine watching a college football game where the players were only interested in advancing the ball if they thought their teammates could be counted on to do their part? Suppose the quarterback would throw the ball to the wide receiver only if he could have assurances in advance that he would catch it. Or suppose the offensive lineman would not defend the quarterback unless he could be convinced that the quarterback would not drop the ball. This clearly sounds like a ridiculous scenario. If college football players acted like that, they would have their scholarships revoked. No team could be expected to win games if the players had such a tenuous trust of their teammates. Now let's look at business in America. How much productivity is lost when team members are not inspired to work hard because they don't see others on the team working hard?

Teams can regain this lost productivity, but leaders must first inspire everyone on the team to believe that everyone else will do what is expected of them. In Chapter 3, a survey respondent wished the boss knew "How their employees act/work when management is not present." That's why this chapter's Culture Health Question is: *Do employees feel that their colleagues are pulling their full weight?*

In the last chapter, I told the story about James Madison University football coach Mike Houston leading the JMU Dukes to a NCAA FCS national championship in his first season there. Coach Houston commented to me about the relationship he developed with his players in that first season: "They trust me because they know there's nothing that I will not do for them. As a result, they will lay it all out there on the field for each other."[1]

> *Everyone you hire is on the team and needs to view themselves as on the team.*

With that said, Coach Houston has created an environment where his players are willing to play to their full potential and trust their teammates to do their job. You can do a similar work in your workplace if you implement three concepts that Mike Houston did with the JMU Dukes.

1. Team Predisposition

Coach Houston wanted to build a team that looked like a team and played like a team. As a result, he had to start with that team predisposition in how he selected the players for his team. He had to look for players who shared that same disposition. And once he selected them for his team, he expected them to act with that same disposition on and off the field.

When you are hiring your team, they have to share the same values of teamwork that you do. If they are not willing to look at themselves and the others with that team disposition, then you should not hire them. You can teach them how to do their job, but you cannot teach them how to have a team disposition.

Everyone you hire is on the team and needs to view themselves as on the team. Even if they are not the ones visible to the customer, they still have to be willing to align their personal goals with the goals of the team. Those who are in support roles have to see how they win when the team wins and lose when the team loses (1 Corinthians 12:26).

2. Consistency of Character

When Coach Houston was building his team, he didn't hold his players to a standard he was not willing to meet himself: "I try to be the person that my players should be. I try to be a man of character."[2] When Coach Houston talks about character, he means a consistency of character: "I haven't wavered. I am the same person who showed up in January 2016."[3]

Your team is looking for you to set the tone. They are looking for you to be the same person tomorrow that you are today. If you will consistently be real with them, they will be inspired to follow you. They will believe what you say when they can see that you are consistent and authentic, day in and day out.

You cannot expect your team to be someone who you are not willing to be yourself. If you are one way on one day, and another way another day, then that lack of consistency will not inspire them to trust you. As the Scripture says, a double-minded man will be unstable in all of his ways (James 1:8).

Your team will be made in your image, whether you like it or not. If you don't like how your team is turning out, then you will need to look in the mirror.

3. Championship-Style Effort

When Coach Houston was in his prior head coaching positions, he had to overcome defeatist attitudes that lingered from his coaching predecessors. He had to get rid of the thinking that settled for just a .500 season. However, winning seasons don't come easily. "We wanted to build a championship culture. That requires giving championship-style effort."[4]

You will not be able to change a losing attitude to a winning attitude overnight. It will take a lot of hard work from you and from your team. However, if you show you are willing to put in the effort, then they will be more willing to do it as well—but they want to see you do it first.

By sharing your vision for where you want to lead your team, and showing them how they can do it, you can inspire them to achieve more than they thought possible. They will want to know that you will be the one leading the charge, working alongside them, and encouraging them. They will want to see that you will be willing to put in that championship-style effort (Ecclesiastes 9:10; Colossians 3:23).

A team mentality doesn't just happen. It has to be carefully cultivated. The people on your team have to believe that if they expend the effort, it won't be for nothing. They have to see that you will be a solid source of strength when things get tough, and that you are willing to put forward the same level of effort that you expect them to put forward.

Reflection Questions

1. Do your team members have a team disposition? Did they have one when you hired them?

2. Would your team say your character consistently inspires them to be who you want them to be?

3. Does your team consistently put forward championship-style effort? Do you?

Notes
_____

1 Coach Mike Houston, telephone interview, May 16, 2017.

2 Ibid.

3 Ibid.

4 Ibid.

CHAPTER 19

Trust

"The best proof of love is trust."

—Joyce Brothers

When I work with heads of companies, I tell them it is their responsibility to set the tone in their business. I tell them that to inspire trust with their team, they have to show by their actions that they walk their talk because their team will be quick to notice when they fall short. I explain that their team will function as the Hypocrisy Police. Whenever the leader's actions veer from what they said should be done, their team will notice. However, their team will usually not tell them that their actions have gone afoul of their words. That's why I tell them that their actions *must* abide by their own rules; otherwise their team will not be able to trust them.

Trust is a fragile thing. No business can survive without it. But what exactly is trust? Here's how Stephen M. R. Covey, author of *The Speed of Trust*, defines it:

> Simply put, trust means *confidence*. The opposite of trust—distrust—is *suspicion*. When you trust people, you have

119

confidence in them—in their integrity and in their abilities. When you distrust people, you are suspicious of them— of their integrity, their agenda, their capabilities, or their track record. It's that simple. We have all had experiences that validate the difference between relationships that are built on trust and those that are not. These experiences clearly tell us the difference is not small; it is dramatic.[1]

Based on what Covey said, I am certain that you can think of times when you were in environments that were built on trust and those that were not. Trust is a huge predictor of the success of the leadership of any business. Therefore, it should be of great concern to us how Gallup's Chairman and CEO Jim Clifton summarized business leadership today: "The very practice of management no longer works."[2] It is equally shocking that Gallup's 2017 *State of the American Workplace* report found that only 22 percent of employees strongly believe their leadership can lead the organization in a clear direction.[3] Leadership in business today is lacking, and employees feel that palpably because they do not trust their leaders.

The good news is that leaders can turn this situation around if they will renew their commitment to their people,[4] but first they need to be willing to do what needs to be done to inspire trust with their team.

Trust is to relationships what oxygen is to life. We are wired to want to trust others, and that is why we are so disappointed when people fail to live up to our expectations. Manager-to-employee relationships cannot function if there is no trust, business-to-customer relationships cannot function if there is no trust, and business-to-business relationships cannot function if there is no trust.

Building trust will be key in moving your business forward. In fact, Steven M. R. Covey says your trustworthiness will be your most important aspect as a leader. *"The ability to establish, grow, extend, and restore trust with all stakeholders—customers, business partners, investors, and coworkers—is the key leadership competency of the new global economy."*[5]

Building trust will require Active Leadership on your part. Remember the Golden Rule (Matthew 7:12). You will need to do for your team what you want your team to do for you. Trust cannot be built in a day. It will take sustained effort over a long period of time to demonstrate that you are

> *Trust is to relationships what oxygen is to life.*

serious about creating a Culture of Trust. You will have to earn the right to be trusted. You will have to show that you are trustworthy. Your team will want to know you—the real you—in order to believe that you are who you say you are. They will want to see that you will do what you will say you will do—over and over again.

In this section, we will explore how Trust will impact your workplace. Over the following five chapters, we will explore the following five topics.

Empowering Employees Allows Trust
Leadership must provide the tools that the team members believe are necessary to do their jobs. It is important to listen to those closest to the job being performed for how the job can be done best.

Inspiring Confidence Activates Trust
Leaders must inspire confidence among the employees in their leaders' ability to run the organization. Even if the leaders are the most qualified in how to run an organization, the team's confidence in their ability to lead must still be actively cultivated.

Exhibiting Fairness Accentuates Trust

Leaders must ensure that they treat all employees fairly. They must have the same standards for measuring everyone's performance, and they must not show partiality or play favorites.

Delegating Decision Making Aggregates Trust

Leadership must provide sufficient autonomy for assignments so that team members can take initiative in their work. Decision making must be decentralized enough for those closest to the work being performed to make the best decisions for the work.

Extending Trust Affords Trust

Leadership must trust their team members will do their best work. Employees should not be micromanaged. Instead, leaders should trust that the team will rise to the occasion and perform their best for the company.

Please let the following chapters sink in. Your ability to build trust with your team will be crucial to your personal success as a leader and to your business's success as well. These concepts will serve to enhance the depth and richness of your relationships with the people you work with, and they will benefit the people who mean the most to you in your personal life as well.

Reflection Questions

1. How trusting do you feel your workplace is?

2. How much have your actions contributed to a Culture of Trust in your workplace?

3. How could you increase the trust that your team has for you? For each other?

Notes

1 Stephen M. R. Covey, *The Speed of Trust: The One Thing That Changes Everything* (New York: Free Press, 2006), 5. Emphasis original.

2 Gallup, Inc., *State of the American Workplace* (Washington, D.C.: Gallup, 2017); accessed at http://www.gallup.com/reports/199961/state-american-workplace-report-2017.aspx.

3 Ibid.

4 Ibid.

5 Stephen M. R. Covey, *The Speed of Trust: The One Thing That Changes Everything* (New York: Free Press, 2006), 21. Emphasis original.

CHAPTER 20

Empowering Employees Allows Trust

"The person who sweeps the floor should choose the broom."

—Howard Behar

When Amazon acquired the internet shoe retailer Zappos in 2009, the deal stipulated that Tony Hsieh and his team would stay on to build the company and to reinforce the culture as well. Hsieh had cultivated a strong company culture at Zappos, ranking in 2010 among the top 15 "Best Companies to Work For" according to *Fortune* magazine. But many feared that Zappos would lose its brand as a result of being assimilated into the internet retailing giant Amazon.

To Amazon's credit, Hsieh was enabled to preserve an independent brand for Zappos. On the one-year anniversary date, he was able to maintain that the brand independence he had promised his team when the acquisition took place was still in force a year later.[1] Amazon understood the value of the Zappos brand, and they also understood that no one could maintain the Zappos brand better than Tony Hsieh. As a result, they ensured Hsieh had the means necessary to guarantee that the brand would remain intact.

Zappos has continued to maintain their brand and culture. For more than a decade, they have offered training to other companies and entrepreneurs to understand how to create a similar environment through Zappos Insights. They transparently teach others how Zappos cultivates their company culture by offering tours, training, and custom events.[2]

Unfortunately, Zappos is not the norm. Too often, the leadership of a company tries to control the means through which their team members are to generate desirable outcomes. They do not always listen to the suggestions that employees will offer to make the process more efficient for the team, or more cost-effective to the customer, or more profitable for the company. As a result, they in effect tell the person who sweeps the floor what kind of broom he should use.

In this chapter, we will explore steps to empower your team to get the job done. In Chapter 4, one survey respondent wanted the boss to know "What exactly I do and how they interfere with the process." That's why this chapter's Culture Health Question is: *Has leadership empowered the team to select the tools that they believe are necessary to do the job?*

By trusting their team members, companies can gain much better outcomes from their employees. Here are three ways that you can prepare your employees to be more successful in their jobs and make the company more successful at the same time.

1. Encourage an ownership mentality.
Let your team "own" what they do. Enable them to see themselves as being fully responsible for what they do. In the case of Tony Hsieh, he needed to have complete control over the Zappos brand

to perpetuate the experience for customers; therefore, he needed to be able to make decisions to preserve and nurture the brand. Because Amazon allowed him to "own" the brand, he could make unfettered decisions to extend the Zappos ideals to the employees and ultimately to their customers.

Former Starbucks President Howard Behar maintains that whoever sweeps the floors must be able to choose the broom because that's how they will get the best results. He believes that the ones who will be held responsible for the results ought to get to choose the means through which they will achieve those results.

> *If your team isn't failing enough, then they are not trying enough.*

Empower your team to make decisions that affect what they do. They know how to do their job better than you do, so encourage them to make decisions in their area of expertise. Giving your team the ability to own what they do will produce better results and will demonstrate that you trust them (Deuteronomy 25:4; 1 Corinthians 9:9; 1 Timothy 5:18).

2. Value your team's input.
If your team tells you they need certain tools or equipment to do their job more effectively, you would be wise to listen to what they say—even if you don't agree with them. If you think that the tools or equipment are not necessary for the job, don't shut down their request automatically. Explain the budget situation to them, identify the approval parameters, and ask for their thoughts. They will be motivated to think through ways to navigate the hurdles to get the approvals and the funds necessary.

Help them to see constraints you have to deal with to comply with their request. Your team may be aware of something you had not considered. By actively soliciting their participation, you will gain more minds to offer specific proposals. You will also create a learning opportunity for leadership training. By encouraging them to consider the same perspectives you do in your leadership role, you will help them to think like a leader. In the process, you will contribute to the company's future success by preparing them to advance up the ranks.

3. Act on your team's recommendations.

Be willing to follow through on what your employees suggest. Even if they make a recommendation that ends up a failure, they will learn from the experience. If your team is not failing enough, then they are not trying enough. It is up to you to help them feel empowered enough to request what they think will best advance the company and best serve the customer. The empowerment process will enable them to have an ownership mentality. They will see how they are active players, and they will realize that they have something to offer because their boss is willing to listen to what they have to say.

The process of listening and acting on what your employees recommend can change the dynamic at your workplace. Knowing that their ideas will be taken seriously will improve their perspective of leadership. They will realize that you are all on the same team. You will benefit by having more engaged employees, they will benefit from the leadership perspective, and the company will benefit by having more of a team environment.

By trusting your employees enough to consider their requests and ideas to improve the company, you will build your team's confidence in themselves. By encouraging an ownership mentality, by making sure that they know that you value their input, and by not second-guessing your team's recommendations, they will see how you have considered them as an active participant—even a partner, of sorts—in actualizing their contributions at the company.

Reflection Questions

1. How can you encourage your team to have more of an ownership mentality?

2. How can you encourage and validate your team's input in order to teach them how to lead?

3. When acting on your team's suggestions doesn't go well, how you can you turn it into a teachable moment— without blaming your employees?

Notes

1 Blake Mycoskie, *Start Something That Matters* (New York: Spiegel & Grau, 2011), 124-125.

2 See Zappos Insights web page, https://www.zapposinsights.com.

CHAPTER 21

Inspiring Confidence
Activates Trust

"Simply put, trust means confidence."
—Stephen M. R. Covey

I travel frequently and I rely on the GPS in my iPhone regularly. When I travel to a new destination, I often don't know where I am going and I implicitly trust that the directions I am getting are correct. One time I drove from my home in the Shenandoah Valley to Virginia Beach. My GPS sent me to the general area where I needed to go, but then it kept sending me in circles. I kept checking the address and repeatedly entering it into the phone, but it kept looping me back to the same area. Frustrated, I finally had to start paying attention to the street signs and navigating myself there without technology. Needless to say, my confidence in my GPS was lessened.

Just like I lost confidence in my GPS, people today have lost confidence in their bosses. In the book *The Speed of Trust*, Stephen M. R. Covey tells us the number one reason people quit their jobs is a poor relationship with their boss.[1] As a result, there are "leading organizations who ask their employees directly the following simple question in formal, 360-degree feedback processes: *'Do you trust your boss?'* These companies have learned that the answer to this one question is more predictive of team and organizational performance than any other question they might ask."[2]

The relationship between employee and boss is greatly significant. The view employees have of management—and their bosses in particular—will shape their view of their job and the entire company. In Chapter 4, a survey respondent said of the boss: "I wish he took responsibility for acting like a manager." It should come as no surprise then that this chapter's Culture Health Question is: *Do employees have confidence that leadership knows how to run the organization?*

> *To be the leader, you don't need to look like the smartest person in the room; instead you need to be the person who is always learning.*

When you are in a leadership role, it is crucial that your team believes in your ability to lead them. That's why you must work with your team in such a way as to inspire confidence in your leadership. Your ability to lead isn't really about what you know. It is more about inspiring them to believe that you have their best interests at heart. Your team will not care how much you know until they know how much you care. You will not inspire confidence in your leadership by being a brash, arrogant, know-it-all boss. Instead you will inspire confidence in your leadership by being an Active Leader.

In order to build a Culture of Trust, here are three things you can do to inspire confidence in your leadership ability.

1. Get to know your team.

We all know from our experience that strangers don't seem as trustworthy as our friends. We might be able to trust strangers, but we can't be sure because we just don't know them. If your team is a collection of people who happen to come to the same place for work day after day, they are not a team; they are strangers who work in the same place. If they do not know each other, they will not trust each other.

Let your team get to know you—not just your professional credentials, but who you are as a person. By knowing the real you, they will develop a deeper trust in your leadership. Tell them your interests. Make sure they know about your family. Help them understand how you think. You can even share with them what you have learned from your failures—so that they don't have to repeat them.

Take the time to get to know your team. Make the environment conducive for them to get to know each other too. Create opportunities for them to work with each other. Have social outings so they can relax around each other. Help them see each other as human beings so they will be more willing to trust each other. They will be more willing to let their guards down around each other if you are willing to let your guard down around them. Of course, it is appropriate to have boundaries between what is private personal information and what is public personal information. Do not share information that you would rather not have publicized outside of your workplace. Nonetheless, the more information you can share about what makes you unique, the more you will appear like a normal person and less like a boss.

2. Admit that you don't know everything.

The more removed you are from the actual work that gets done, the more your team knows that you don't know what they know. It's okay to admit to your team that you don't know it. That may be a hard thing to admit, but they already know. Why not just say the obvious? By being open about something you don't know, they will have a newfound appreciation for your leadership. By admitting that you don't know everything, your team will respect you more. (Matthew 23:12; Luke 14:11; 1 Peter 5:6)

You might think that admitting what you don't know exposes you as being vulnerable. Actually, your team will see you as being real with them. That vulnerability will endear you to your team because they will know you are telling them the truth. To be the leader, you don't need to look like the smartest person in the room; instead you need to be the person who is always learning. It's okay to be humble and ask for your team's suggestions. Ask how you could be a better boss. Ask how you could be a greater resource to them. Ask how you can serve them better as a leader. Ask them for their thoughts on big decisions you need to make. They may well have an answer for you, and you may be surprised by what you will learn.

By admitting that you don't know everything and by involving your team in solving company problems, they will respect your leadership all the more.

3. Explain important decisions.

If you ask your team's advice when you are making big decisions, make sure you genuinely consider their input, and then tell them what you end up deciding. If you don't end up doing what they recommend, it is important to explain your decision fully. Help them understand what went into your decision making so they don't come up with their own conclusions. If you don't tell them why you decided what you did, it will be worse than if you hadn't asked for their input at all; they will think that you weren't really interested what they had to say.

Be willing to answer questions from your team, especially if your decisions have an impact on their employment or compensation. You may even have to field some questions or comments that will seem antagonistic. Do not be intimidated. Help them see that your decision making had their wellbeing in mind, and their best interests at heart.

You can improve your team's confidence in your leadership ability by getting to know your team, admitting you don't know everything, and explaining the decisions you make. They want to know that you consider them as part of the team and that you do not elevate yourself above the team. As counterintuitive as it may be, the more humility you exhibit as a leader to your team, the more you will be able to inspire confidence in your leadership ability.

Reflection Questions

1. How can you create opportunities for your team to get to know you—and each other?

2. How can you make a habit of asking your team for their advice?

3. How can you create a forum to explain important decisions you have made?

Notes

1 Stephen M. R. Covey, *The Speed of Trust: The One Thing That Changes Everything* (New York: Free Press, 2006), 12.

2 Ibid., 17. Emphasis original.

CHAPTER 22

Exhibiting Fairness Accentuates Trust

"Fairness is not an attitude. It's a professional skill that must be developed and exercised."

—Brit Hume

In the biblical account, Jacob loved his son Joseph more than any of his other children. Joseph was born when Jacob was old, and Joseph was the firstborn of his favorite (and deceased) wife. Because Joseph was his favorite son, Jacob gave Joseph a special robe, which made his brothers jealous. After Joseph told on his brothers, they hated him and couldn't say anything good about him. One time when Joseph came to check up on his brothers, they conspired to get rid of him and sold him as a slave to traveling merchants (Genesis 37).

This perceived unfairness had dire consequences in Jacob's family, and perceived unfairness will have dire consequences in your business as well. John Mackey and Raj Sisodia point out in *Conscious Capitalism* that "trust quickly unravels when there is a perception of unfairness. Human beings have a strong need to be respected, heard, and treated fairly. Research has shown that most people would rather have a fair and transparent process for making decisions, even if it leads to an unfavorable outcome for them personally, than an unfair process that may result in a positive outcome for them."[1]

Fairness is a crucial piece of creating a Culture of Trust, and your employees will be extremely sensitized to what they deem to be fair. In Chapter 4, one of the survey respondents wished the boss had the "Ability to be non bias [sic]." Along those lines, the Culture Health Question for this chapter is: *Do employees believe that leadership treats everyone fairly?*

In order to develop a Culture of Trust, it is important to think through not only what is fair to everyone, but what is beneficial to the entire team. Here are three things to consider.

1. Do not play favorites.

As a leader, you have to work through your team to accomplish results. Over time, you may have come to rely on certain performers on your team. As helpful and as reliable as they may be, it is important that you not play favorites (Proverbs 24:23; Romans 2:11; James 2:1). While you may be able to rationalize why you favor some people more than others, it is imperative to think through the unintended consequences that can happen, as they did to Jacob.

By playing favorites, you may make some on your team feel more important, but you run the risk of alienating the rest of your team. If they perceive that you are unfair in how you look at the members of the team, they will not trust you as a leader.

Your organization will benefit the most when you seek to create a Culture of Trust. Everything you do as a leader should be focused on fostering an environment of trust. If you play favorites, you will not develop an environment that is perceived as fair, and it will not encourage trust on your team. Instead you will compromise your efforts to create a Culture of Trust for those who fall outside your favored group. In effect, you will create a tiered organization with some who are the favored class, and some who are not.

2. Use the same standards.

In the workplace, everyone should be made aware of what the standards are and what the expectations are. To be fair, everyone should have the same opportunity to perform at their jobs. When assessing the team, the same standards should apply for everyone to ensure that the process is fair (Deuteronomy 25:15; Proverbs 20:10).

It is important not only to be impartial about individual team members, but to also have a system that is impartial. Make sure that you have a performance review perspective that will allow for consistency. Being conscious of any personal biases you may have will help you make your system beneficial to everyone. If your goal is to develop a Culture of Trust in the team, providing a system that can provide checks and balances to your personal preferences will produce an environment of fairness.

It is one thing for you to have a personal practice of impartiality, but it is another to make sure that it takes hold in your organization.

3. Do not condone partiality.

It is imperative to be conscious of how you personally perceive others in order to ensure fairness at your workplace. Taking that further, creating a system for impartiality will perpetuate that environment of fairness. In addition, your vigilance in rooting out any playing of favorites will serve to institutionalize a Culture of Trust at your workplace.

It is one thing for you to have a personal practice of impartiality, but it is another to make sure that it takes hold in your organization. You will need to be watchful to prevent any of your team leaders or team members from playing favorites. Condoning a practice of partiality—or the appearance of condoning this practice—will be detrimental to creating a Culture of Trust.

Your workplace is looking for you to provide a place where everyone can contribute to the organization (Colossians 4:1; 1 Timothy 5:21). You can create a workplace culture that is beneficial to everyone by treating your team with the same fairness with which you would want to be treated (Matthew 7:12), by creating an environment where everyone can stand on their own merits, and by ridding the company of practices of partiality.

Reflection Questions

1. How can you create a Culture of Trust that is truly fair to everyone on your team?

2. How can you develop a standard that everyone on the team will appreciate?

3. How can you create an environment that is beneficial to all concerned?

Notes

1 John Mackey and Raj Sisodia, *Conscious Capitalism: Liberating the Heroic Spirit of Business* (Boston: Harvard Business School Publishing Corporation, 2014), 224.

CHAPTER 23

Decentralizing Decision Making Aggregates Trust

"Initiative is doing the right thing without being told."

—Victor Hugo

Before the invention of electronic tickets, a customer shopping at Nordstrom accidentally left at the counter her airline ticket for a flight she was going to take later that day. A sales associate noticed the ticket and immediately called the airline to determine if the passenger could be located and the ticket reissued. Upon hearing that was not possible, the Nordstrom associate caught a cab to the airport, paid the cab fare, located the traveler, and personally delivered the ticket. Not only did Nordstrom reimburse the cab fare, the company endorsed her actions—because it was the Nordstrom way.[1]

Nordstrom became famous for their customer service policy. In fact, they became known for being better at customer service than all other retailers. How? Robert Spector and Patrick McCarthy explain in *The Nordstrom Way*: "Nordstrom's culture encourages entrepreneurial, motivated men and women to make the extra effort to give customer service that is unequalled in American retailing."[2]

Nordstrom has a section in their Code of Business Conduct and Ethics entitled "**USE GOOD JUDGMENT IN ALL SITUATIONS**" (emphasis original), and they expect employees "to use good judgment when it comes to taking care of our customers and in your interactions with other Nordstrom employees and vendors. ... When we talk about using good judgment, it's really about how we treat our customers, how we treat each other and how we do business."[3]

In Scripture, Moses learned a lesson about decentralizing decision making from his father-in-law when Jethro visited him in the wilderness. Jethro saw the people standing around Moses all day long to have Moses decide their disputes, and Jethro saw there was a better way.

> You shall represent the people before God and bring their cases to God, and you shall warn them about the statutes and the laws, and make them know the way in which they must walk and what they must do. Moreover, look for able men from all the people, men who fear God, who are trustworthy and hate a bribe, and place such men over the people as chiefs of thousands, of hundreds, of fifties, and of tens. And let them judge the people at all times. Every great matter they shall bring to you, but any small matter they shall decide themselves. So it will be easier for you, and they will bear the burden with you (Exodus 18:19b-22).

Jethro taught Moses that everyone would be better served by decentralizing decision-making authority and giving the people the autonomy to decide issues that more directly affected them. In your business, you can develop a Culture of Trust by giving your team the autonomy to make decisions that will best serve the interests of customers—and ultimately, the company.

On the other hand, micromanaging your team will prevent that Culture of Trust from forming. In Chapter 4, one survey respondent wanted the boss to know "I know how to do my job so micro managing [sic] is unnecessary." It makes sense that this chapter's Culture Health Question would be: *Does leadership provide sufficient autonomy for assignments so workers can take initiative in their work?*

By building a Culture of Trust, you will encourage your team to become entrepreneurial. To understand how giving your team autonomy will build a Culture of Trust, here are three points you can consider.

> *You will best serve the company if you give your team the freedom to fail.*

1. Allow your team to fail.

In order for your team to become successful, they need to have enough autonomy to make decisions on their own. Most of the time, they will probably make good decisions. However, every now and then, they will make bad decisions. You will best serve the company if you give your team the freedom to fail. It's been said that if you are not failing enough, then you are not trying enough. If you are not allowing your team to gain experience from trying new things, then they will never rise to the level of their best work. That requires failing along the way.

Innovation happens when people feel free enough to exercise their good judgment without fear of reprisal (1 John 4:18). People will do the right things more often than not when they are expected to use good judgment.

As I have stated earlier, it is incumbent on you to hire the right people for your positions. If you do not have the right people in the right positions at your company, then these principles will not apply.

Only by hiring the right people who will fit your values and culture will you have team members who will abide by your values and culture.

2. Permit your team to grow.

When you allow your team to fail, you will encourage your team to take initiative—solely because you are trusting them. People will act more trustworthily when they are trusted. That means letting go of a mentality of control and any tendency to micromanage. Blake Mycoskie, the founder and Chief Shoe Giver at TOMS, says in *Start Something That Matters* that micromanaging will kill initiative: "When you micromanage, you're effectively telling people that you don't trust their judgment and that, unless you're personally involved in every detail, the project won't get done right."[4]

The responsibility and burden of micromanaging your team will wear you out, like it did for Moses. Not only will micromanaging stifle any creativity, it will sap your energy. The best option is to trust your people and trust their judgment. Your team will fail, and your team will learn; as a result, your team will grow.

3. Stick by your team.

The most important part of allowing your team to fail and permitting your team to grow is sticking by your team. They need to know that you will defend them if they try new things. I heard a story about a young executive who, early on in his career, made a mistake that cost his company $2 million. After worriedly putting together his resume, he went into his boss' office to tender his resignation. At this action, his boss was incredulous: "I just invested $2 million in your training and you are going to resign?!" The young executive's boss understood that he had to give him enough latitude to fail in order for him to learn how to succeed.

The Nordstrom sales associate (mentioned at the beginning of the chapter) knew that her company prided themselves on their customer service, so she was willing to do what many other companies would have called a fool's errand. That's how Nordstrom became known for customer service.

By extending trust to your team, they will rise to the challenge. Let your team experiment. Allow them to make mistakes. Give them the opportunity to grow. In the process of failing and learning, your team will gain a confidence in themselves that they would not have been able to gain any other way. The lessons they learn will be more memorable than anything they could ever read out of a book, and the loyalty they develop will be unswerving if you remain loyal to them when they fail. It all starts with you as an Active Leader setting the tone and giving them the autonomy to take entrepreneurial initiative in their work.

Reflection Questions

1. How comfortable are you with the idea of allowing your team to fail?

2. How can you give your team opportunities to experiment?

3. How can you let your team know you will stick with them if things don't go as planned?

Notes

1 Robert Spector and Patrick D. McCarthy, *The Nordstrom Way: The Inside Story of America's #1 Customer Service Company* (New York: John Wiley & Sons, 1995), 125.

2 Ibid., 1.

3 Nordstrom, *Code of Business Conduct and Ethics*, Amended and Restated on May 5, 2017; accessed at http://investor.nordstrom.com/phoenix. zhtml?c=93295&p=irol-govconduct.

4 Blake Mycoskie, *Start Something That Matters* (New York: Spiegel & Grau, 2011), 146.

CHAPTER 24

Extending Trust Affords Trust

"The productivity of work is not the responsibility
of the worker but of the manager."

—Peter Drucker

"Julie" has worked as a reservationist part-time for JetBlue for 17 years from home. She appreciates the trust that JetBlue leadership has placed in her and her fellow reservationists. She does not take lightly the trust offered her to work from home. When the weather outside is bad, she finds it comforting that she does not have to go out in it in order to do her work.[1]

JetBlue does not have a call center where all their reservations are handled; instead calls are taken by reservationists in their own homes. While their training takes place in a centralized location, team members then take their computers home to get their work done remotely. As discerned in my conversation with "Julie," I could not tell by any external evidence that she worked from home, and she was as courteous as—if not more courteous than—those who work in a centralized location.

> *In order to instill trust into your team, your team will need to know that you trust them.*

JetBlue seems to understand the wisdom behind the Golden Rule: Do to others what you would want them to do to you (Matthew 7:12)—or in this case, to customers. Based on my conversation with "Julie," that rings true.

As "Julie" stated in my conversation with her, JetBlue reservationists appreciate the trust extended to them. Because they are trusted to do their jobs, even when they cannot be observed, they want to live up to the trust extended to them.

In Chapter 4, one of the survey respondents wanted the boss to know that "People under him are working for the best for the company." That's why this chapter's Culture Health Question is: *Do employees believe that leadership trusts them to produce a good work product?*

Leadership must trust that their team members want to do their best work. In order to demonstrate that kind of trust with your team, here are three points you can put into practice in your own company.

1. Believe in your team.
Trust is a powerful motivator. Choose to believe the best about your employees. Tell them that you trust them. Then demonstrate that you trust them.

Nehemiah believed that his people could rebuild the wall of Jerusalem. Nehemiah was moved by how Jerusalem was in ruins. He prayed that God would give him favor with King Artaxerxes as his cupbearer to go to Jerusalem and rebuild the city wall. After the king granted his request, he assessed the situation upon his arrival in

Jerusalem (Nehemiah 1:1-16). When he reported his findings to the people, he told them he believed they could get the work done.

> "You see the trouble we are in, how Jerusalem lies in ruins with its gates burned. Come, let us build the wall of Jerusalem, that we may no longer suffer derision." And I told them of the hand of my God that had been upon me for good, and also of the words that the king had spoken to me. And they said, "Let us rise up and build." So they strengthened their hands for the good work (Nehemiah 2:17-18).

The people responded positively to Nehemiah's belief that they could rebuild the wall. Similarly, your employees will want to show you that you have made a good decision in giving them your trust. They will want to perform to your expectations to show you that you can continue to extend your trust to them.

Think through situations where you can extend trust to your team. Can you allow your employees to set their own schedules? Can you give your team performance standards and then let them run with them? Can you give them the latitude to be independent and check in only when they need help? The belief that you have in them will be reciprocated as well. They will end up believing more in you and in your leadership too.

2. Rely on your team.
Believing in your team is good, but relying on your team is better. Reliance is one step beyond belief. When you rely on your team, you show them that they must rise to the occasion because *your* actions are dependent on *their* actions.

Nehemiah relied on the people to complete rebuilding the wall, even when they were flagging in their faith that it could be done.

In Judah it was said, "The strength of those who bear the burdens is failing. There is too much rubble. By ourselves we will not be able to rebuild the wall." ... So in the lowest parts of the space behind the wall, in open places, I stationed the people by their clans, with their swords, their spears, and their bows. And I looked and arose and said to the nobles and to the officials and to the rest of the people, "Do not be afraid of them. Remember the Lord, who is great and awesome, and fight for your brothers, your sons, your daughters, your wives, and your homes" (Nehemiah 4:10, 13-14).

Nehemiah counteracted the people's complaints by reminding them that others depended on their successful completion of the wall. In your workplace, even if people on your team have been critical of your actions as a leader, your reliance on them empowers them to act more like leaders. They can no longer afford to be critical; they are now in a position where they must prove themselves to be reliable.

Can you rely on your team to do what's necessary without requiring your involvement? To prepare things for your approval that don't require your review? To represent you, your boss, or your company without hesitation? Reliance demonstrates your trust at a higher level. It shows your team that you are serious about trusting them.

3. Have confidence in the team's work.
Relying on your team will show how much you believe in them. Showing that you are confident in the work your team produces will transform them.

Nehemiah was confident that the people could complete the wall. After only 52 days, despite threats from enemies and lack of confidence, they finished rebuilding the wall (Nehemiah 6:15).

Stand by your team's work in front of others. Let them know that you fully believe in the quality of the work they do. Your team wants to do good work. They will want to maintain that level of excellence when you tell others how good your team is at doing the work they do.

In what ways can you express your confidence in your team? Could you give them an aggressive growth goal and know that they could meet it? Could you take off for a month and be confident that they would not need you? Could you find your successor among the ranks of your team?

If you hired your team and you trained your team, it only makes sense that you would believe in your team. However, it will take more than words to convince them that you trust them. They will need to see it in your actions.

In order to instill trust into your team, your team will need to know that you trust them. Let them know you believe in them. Let them know that you are counting on them. Say in front of others that you trust them to produce a good work product. You may be surprised how much that extension of trust can transform your team.

Reflection Questions

1. How can you demonstrate trust in your team by your leadership actions?

2. How can you show by your actions that you rely on your team?

3. In what ways can you express your confidence in your team?

Notes

1 "Julie" (JetBlue reservationist), telephone interview, May 24, 2017.

CHAPTER 25

Transparency

"I think the currency of leadership is transparency."

—Howard Schultz

Jesus and his disciples were gathered around the supper table before the Passover Feast. Jesus got up from the table, took off his outer garments, and wrapped himself with a towel. He poured water in a basin and started washing the disciples' feet and drying their feet with the towel around his waist. When it was Simon Peter's turn, Peter was incredulous that his master would wash his feet.

> He came to Simon Peter, who said to him, "Lord, do you wash my feet?" Jesus answered him, "What I am doing you do not understand now, but afterward you will understand." Peter said to him, "You shall never wash my feet." Jesus answered him, "If I do not wash you, you have no share with me." Simon Peter said to him, "Lord, not my feet only but also my hands and my head!" (John 13:6-9).

Simon Peter was an impetuous disciple of Jesus, but he was transparent. Very possibly the other disciples thought the same thing that Peter did, but he was the only one who said anything.

As Stephen M. R. Covey defines it in *The Speed of Trust*, transparency "is about being open. It's about being real and genuine and telling the truth."[1] Ultimately, transparency is communication between parties that engenders a Culture of Tenderness, Team, and Trust. As Blake Mycoskie explains in *Start Something That Matters*, "Revealing your true self makes you more real to everyone around you. And the more real you are, the more they'll trust you."[2]

With most people, this scenario seems unreal. Many people have an intense fear that they will be exposed as a fraud. As a result, they have no interest in revealing their true selves. In fact, they do everything they can to hide who they really are. This fearful behavior is not healthy. Similarly, organizations that do not have a policy of transparency are not healthy. As John Mackey and Raj Sisodia wisely understand in *Conscious Capitalism*, "cultures of organizations that have virtually no transparency usually have a great deal of fear."[3] Fear and distrust do not produce positive cultures (1 John 4:18).

Most communication scenarios are designed to conceal information rather than disclose it. When a couple is dating, most of their time together seems to be designed to position themselves in the best light, rather than to share information transparently with someone who may become their future spouse. When an applicant comes in for a job interview, he reveals only the amount of information that will help him secure the job—especially if the information he conceals would show he and the company would be a bad fit for each other. When unions and management are in contract negotiations, both sides try to get the most out of the situation, and they will reveal only what they perceive will benefit their side. As a result, transparency is not the norm.

> *Transparency is to relationships as oil is to an engine.*

It should be no surprise then that Gallup found that the information flow from team leaders to team members is not perceived to be good. Gallup's 2017 *State of the American Workplace* report said that only one out of eight employees "strongly agree the leadership of their organization communicates effectively with the rest of the organization."[4] However, it doesn't have to be this way.

The good news about transparency is that both sides don't have to initiate transparent communication. One party can choose to be transparent, and that can change the entire tenor of the conversation and the relationship.

Being transparent begins with realizing that you can have better-quality communications and better-quality relationships when you are willing to be open and clear. To be sure, transparency presents a certain amount of risk, but the benefits of transparent and healthy communication far outweigh the risks in terms of how much interpersonal relations will improve. As Mackey and Sisodia explain, "we live in an increasingly transparent world in which most information of genuine significance soon becomes known. Conscious firms embrace this reality and benefit from it."[5]

Transparency is to relationships as oil is to an engine. When communication between parties is transparent, then the walls come down, the relationship solidifies, and a Culture of Tenderness, Team, and Trust flourish.

In this section, we will explore how Transparency will impact your workplace. In the following five chapters, we will discuss the following five topics.

Demonstrating Authenticity Exhibits Transparency

Leadership must communicate authentically with the team. It is important that team leaders are genuine with team members so that they feel they are getting accurate information.

Creating Clarity Expects Transparency

Leadership must clarify expectations so that everyone on the team understands their responsibilities. The clearer the expectations are, the more likely it is that a positive outcome will result.

Understanding Others Encourages Transparency

Leadership must ensure that communications with the team are understood by everyone. Not only must everyone be able to speak, but everyone must be willing to listen and then clarify that they understand.

Sharing Information Elicits Transparency

Leadership must freely share information. There must be a free flow of information from team leaders to team members so they feel they are being included and not excluded from the information flow.

Meeting Face to Face Extends Transparency

Leadership must be willing to share information in person. Information without facial and verbal contextualization is subject to rumors. Face-to-face sharing of information will help the team feel included and not excluded.

By improving the openness, tenor, and format of their communications, leadership can radically transform the workplace and their relationships with employees. The flow of information can serve to be an antidote to the poisonous interpersonal dynamics that have been killing Tenderness, Team, and Trust over the years.

Read, process, and possibly re-read this section. I understand that these practices may be completely contrary to what you have been accustomed to doing for years, and perhaps decades. It will take time to implement these ideas and it will take time to see the changes. But you will reap great professional and personal rewards if you persevere and do what the following chapters suggest.

Reflection Questions

1. How much transparency do you have in your organization now?

2. How much have your actions contributed to a Culture of Transparency? How have they not?

3. How could you become more transparent in your communications with your team?

Notes

1 Stephen M. R. Covey, *The Speed of Trust: The One Thing That Changes Everything* (New York: Free Press, 2006), 153.

2 Blake Mycoskie, *Start Something That Matters* (New York: Spiegel & Grau, 2011), 145.

3 John Mackey and Raj Sisodia, *Conscious Capitalism: Liberating the Heroic Spirit of Business* (Boston: Harvard Business School Publishing Corporation, 2014), 224.

4 Gallup, Inc., *State of the American Workplace* (Washington, D.C.: Gallup, 2017); accessed at http://www.gallup.com/reports/199961/state-american-workplace-report-2017.aspx.

5 John Mackey and Raj Sisodia, *Conscious Capitalism: Liberating the Heroic Spirit of Business* (Boston: Harvard Business School Publishing Corporation, 2014), 219.

CHAPTER 26

Demonstrating Authenticity Exhibits Transparency

*"I know of nothing more valuable, when it comes
to the all-important virtue of authenticity,
than simply being who you are."*

—Chuck Swindoll

When Philip told Nathanael that he had found the one the prophets had written about—and that he was from Nazareth—Nathanael asked Philip if anything good could come from Nazareth. While watching Nathanael approach, Jesus said to him, "Behold, an Israelite indeed, in whom there is no deceit!" Despite Nathanael's derogatory statement about Jesus's hometown, Jesus was apparently pleased by Nathanael's authenticity. He knew that Nathanael would be up front with him (John 1:45-47).

In today's business culture, we have grown accustomed to people not being up front with us. It seems commonplace to feel like we're being deceived. Claims are made that exaggerate the facts, and the

> *The fastest way to earn trust with your team is to be real with them.*

line that divides truth from lies is often blurred. However, today more than ever, people crave authenticity. They want to know that you are who you say you are. Therefore, it is imperative that you have an authenticity mindset with your team.

In Chapter 5, one of the survey respondents wanted to tell leadership "How they are really perceived." That's why this chapter's Culture Health Question is: *Do employees believe that leadership consistently communicates in an authentic manner?*

Your team will want to believe you, but they are used to being conned. You will have to surmount their jaundiced view of management. Here are three ways you can overcome distrust by developing a practice of authenticity.

1. Be open.

If you want to be trusted, then you must show yourself trustworthy. A good way to do that is to be open. Share your thoughts so your team knows where you're coming from. That way you can build a relationship based on open communication.

Remember to live by the Golden Rule (Matthew 7:12). Try to think through how you would feel if you were in their place. That will help you to realize the high value your team will place on your openness. If you had a boss who never communicated with you, you would never be able to read her. You would never know what she was thinking. You would never know if she was pleased with you or not. That would be would a very frustrating experience. You would be tempted to assume what she was thinking, even if you were incorrect in your assumption—only because she wasn't open with you.

Make sure your team knows where you're coming from. Tell them what your leadership perspective is. Be quick to let them know what you're thinking. Make sure they know where they stand with you. By being more open with your team, they will feel more comfortable about being open with you.

2. Be real.
The fastest way to earn trust with your team is to be real with them. By dropping your guard around them, they will feel like they can drop their guard around you. That will help you develop a relational framework upon which you can build your professional communications.

When you are sharing with your team how best to do something, don't just use a manual. Tell your team about the times you have messed up—and what you learned from your mistakes. Share some embarrassing moments with your team when you didn't do something the right way. They will remember the context of the lesson better because the stories will make a strong impression with them.

Your team wants to be led, but they want to be led by someone they can trust; they will feel like they can trust you if you are real.

3. Be truthful.
Telling the truth to your team will help you develop a healthy channel of communication. If they know you will tell them the truth, they will be more likely to believe you. The key is that you must tell the truth *all* the time, not just some of the time. If you are not truthful all the time, your team will never know when they can trust you.

You will want to tell your team the truth, not just what you think they want to hear. It is easy to have the impression that people don't want to hear the hard truth. We tend to think that we will develop the relationship better if we sugarcoat the situation. Actually, your team would rather hear the hard truth and then get it over with than to be fed an untruth that they discover later wasn't the real story. In addition, not telling the hard truth early will ultimately damage your relationship with your team.

Develop a policy of authenticity with your team. Be willing to be open and real and truthful with them. Help them to see that you are who you are all the time, and that you will share the real story with them all the time. If you do that, they will want to follow you all the time.

Reflection Questions

1. How can you develop a practice of openness with your team?

2. In what ways can you show the real you to your team?

3. Do you need to adjust your communication style to be more authentic?

CHAPTER 27

Creating Clarity
Expects Transparency

"Clarity affords focus."

—Thomas Leonard

In John's Gospel, Jesus gave a blind man sight. After spitting on the ground and making mud with the saliva, Jesus placed the mud on the man's eyes. Then Jesus told him to wash his eyes in the pool of Siloam. After he washed his eyes, he came back seeing. Later, Jesus asked him if he believed in the Son of Man. The formerly blind man asked who the Son of Man was that he might believe in him. Jesus told him that the Son of Man was the one who was speaking to him, and the man believed in him and worshipped him (John 9:6-7, 35-38).

Jesus gave the man clarity on two levels: he gave him physical sight as well as spiritual sight. Before Jesus washed his eyes, the man could not see the world around him nor the more important spiritual truths Jesus was imparting. As a result of what Jesus did, the man said: "One thing I do know, that though I was blind, now I see" (John 9:25b).

Similarly, clarity is one of the greatest gifts you can give your team. Everyone needs to have expectations clarified, and it's important to think through what can get in the way of having those expectations clarified. By removing the hindrances to clear communications, your team will gain clarity about what is expected of them. Otherwise, in the absence of clear expectations, your team will make assumptions that may not be realized. In that environment, problems are sure to follow.

In the absence of clear expectations, your team will make assumptions that may not be realized. In that environment, problems are sure to follow.

You can help everyone understand your perspective by thinking through what you want to communicate and then how you communicate it. When communicating with your team, it is important to be clear in what you trying to say as well as in how you are trying to say it.

In Chapter 5, one of the respondents wished the boss knew the "details of responsibility sharing with other department teams." To address this issue, this chapter's Culture Health Question is: *Have expectations been clarified so that everyone understands their responsibilities?*

Here are three steps to clarifying expectations so that everything is out in the open and you have transparent communications with your team.

1. Articulate expectations.

Whether your team has been in place for a long time or it has been newly formed, it is always good to articulate your expectations for everyone's responsibilities.

- When you have new hires, detail their responsibilities in a job description—but don't stop there. Make sure you commit to writing what your expectations are. Describe for them what a good job looks like. Help them to understand what you as the leader are expecting.

- If you and your team have not worked together before—or if someone new has recently joined your team—formalizing your expectations is always prudent. Set the tone for how the group should function together. Put it in writing so that everyone on the team can reference it.

- Even if your team has been in place for a long time, spelling out expectations will help you circumvent misunderstandings. Over time, people can have unspoken—and unmet—expectations that create friction on the team and in the workplace.

By clarifying those expectations for everyone on your team, you can clear up confusion before it happens and create a Culture of Transparency.

2. Anticipate concerns.

After you articulate your expectations, think through what concerns your team may have. List potential objections your team may raise and identify how to address those concerns. Help them to see that your expectations are reasonable and why they are important. Then use the Golden Rule (Matthew 7:12) and put yourself in their place. If you were in their shoes, how would you interpret your expectations? If your expectations don't seem as reasonable from their vantage point, you will want to adjust your expectations accordingly. Only when you put yourself in the place of others will your expectations seem reasonable to others.

It's important for you to have insight into what it will be like to operate under your expectations. Make sure you are willing to gain clarity by looking at the situation from your team's vantage point.

3. Communicate clearly.

Your words have to mean what you think they mean (Matthew 5:37). Use words that are clear to everyone in your communications, whether in writing or in conversation. If you are using terminology or vocabulary that your team isn't familiar with, define it for them. Don't leave the interpretation of your words up to them.

Do not hurry to communicate information to your team. When sending emails, re-read what you've written to make sure it makes sense. If it is unclear, then start over again. It is always better to take the time up front to explain what you mean. When you're talking on the phone or in person, make sure you are being clear in what you're saying. Do not rush through your words. Clearly enunciate everything you say so that it can be clearly understood.

Be transparent in your communications. Don't have any hidden meanings in what you're trying to say. Remember, to be unclear is to be unkind. By articulating your expectations, anticipating your team's concerns, and communicating clearly, you will create a Culture of Transparency.

Reflection Questions

1. How can you clarify your expectations for the different people on your team?

2. If you were in your team members' shoes, how would you react to your expectations?

3. Are you aware of how your written or verbal communications are received and perceived?

CHAPTER 28

Understanding Others
Encourages Transparency

*"When you really listen to another person from their point
of view, and reflect back to them that understanding,
it's like giving them emotional oxygen."*

—Stephen R. Covey

One of the most famous comedy sketches of all time is "Who's on
First?" performed by Bud Abbott and Lou Costello. In their routine,
Lou asks Bud the names of the players on the St. Louis baseball team.
Bud tells him what their unconventional names are (Who, What, and
I Don't Know), but Lou still doesn't understand. Despite how much
Bud tries to explain the names to Lou, he still doesn't understand.
Lou's paradigm for baseball players' names does not include names
like "Who," "What," and "I Don't Know." Without a paradigm shift,
Lou will never understand what Bud is trying to tell him.

As ridiculous and comical as this sketch is, similar conversations
take place in businesses all the time, except these impasses are not as
funny. Two sides have carved out their diametrically opposite opinions,

and neither wants to give any ground. And even more disappointing is that neither side wants to genuinely listen to the other.

Without genuinely listening, no forward movement in relationships can occur. Genuine listening, or what Stephen R. Covey called "empathic listening" in *The 7 Habits of Highly Effective People*, is essential to creating an environment where understanding between parties can occur.

> You have to build the skills of empathic listening on a base of character that inspires openness and trust. And you have to build the Emotional Bank Accounts that create a commerce between hearts. …
>
> When I say empathic listening, I mean listening with intent to *understand*. I mean *seeking first* to understand, to really understand. It's an entirely different paradigm.
>
> Empathic (from *empathy*) listening gets inside another person's frame of reference. You look out through it, you see the world the way they see the world, you understand their paradigm, you understand how they feel …
>
> Empathic listening is, in and of itself, a tremendous deposit in the Emotional Bank Account. It's deeply therapeutic and healing because it gives a person "psychological air."[1]

When you empathically listen to someone, without trying to manipulate them, you give the other person "psychological air" or "emotional oxygen." You have met one of their deeply felt needs—the need to be understood. When you genuinely listen to someone, you provide fertile ground for transparency to grow. It is through that environment of listening and transparency that understanding will flourish.

In Chapter 5, a survey respondent wished the boss knew "How to communicate effectively." As a result, this chapter's Culture Health Question is: *Are communications between leadership and employees characterized by mutual understanding?*

Here are three practical ways to foster mutual understanding with the people you work with.

1. Don't Assume.

When you talk to someone else, do you assume that you know what they will say? You may not think that you do that intentionally. However, do your actions betray your attitude?

I went to a conference where one of the presenters was a "kid" who was barely half my age. At first, I assumed that I had more to teach him because I

> *When you genuinely listen to someone, you provide fertile ground for transparency to grow.*

was old enough to be his father. As it turned out, I learned more from him at that conference than any other presenter. I had to put my assumptions on hold. I found I had to make a paradigm shift and put myself in the student role and him in the teacher role. I had to admit that my assumptions about him were wrong.

Do you make assumptions about the people on your team? Do you think they are always going to say the same things? Be careful to jump to conclusions. You may be wrong about them.

2. Always Be Learning.

I have realized in my life that I am not learning when I am talking. I have two ears and one mouth. I should use them in proportion. If I had talked and not listened to this kid at the conference, I would not have benefited from the knowledge he had to share. I had to be quiet, listen, and learn.

Be humble enough to learn from others (Matthew 23:12; Luke 14:11; 1 Peter 5:6). Take time to listen to somebody else, even if you don't think you can learn anything from them. In fact, listen to them *especially* if you don't think you can learn anything from them. You may be surprised by what you will learn.

3. Verify Your Interpretations.

Even when you have listened to the other party, go back to Point #1: Don't assume that you have heard them correctly. Take the time to share what you think you heard to make sure that you have understood them. Then let them confirm what is accurate and correct what is not.

By showing that you genuinely want to understand them, you will demonstrate that you are someone they can work with. Your actions will say so much more than any persuasive words you could say. As a result, you will forge a path for future transparent communications.

By not assuming, you will start you on a good footing with any relationship. By making the effort to learn what the other party genuinely thinks and feels, you will solidify that relationship. Through taking the time to verify you understand their position, you will etch your goodwill permanently in their minds.

Reflection Questions

1. What do your actions say about the assumptions you make concerning your team members?

2. How much of the time do you talk? How much do you listen? What is the ratio between them?

3. How often do you take the time to verify your interpretations of what your team tells you?

Notes

1 Stephen R. Covey, *The 7 Habits of Highly Effective People: Powerful Lessons in Personal Change* (New York: Fireside, 1990), 239-241. Emphasis original.

CHAPTER 29

Sharing Information Elicits Transparency

"More information is always better than less. When people know the reason things are happening, even if it's bad news, they can adjust their expectations and react accordingly."

—Simon Sinek

In his book *Start with Why*, Simon Sinek begins the first chapter with this description.

> On a cold January day, a forty-three-year-old man was sworn in as the chief executive of his country. By his side stood his predecessor, a famous general who, fifteen years earlier, had commanded his nation's armed forces in a war that resulted in the defeat of Germany. The young leader was raised in the Roman Catholic faith. He spent the next five

> hours watching parades in his honor and
> stayed up celebrating until three o'clock in
> the morning.
>
> You know who I'm describing, right?
>
> It's January 30, 1933, and I'm describing Adolf Hitler and
> not, as most people would assume, John F. Kennedy.[1]

Without the key piece of information of the date this event took place, you probably assumed incorrectly who Simon Sinek was talking about. Without that information, you were forced to make an assumption. As Sinek says, "[w]e make assumptions about the world around us based on sometimes incomplete or false information. ... This is important because our behavior is affected by our assumptions or our perceived truths."[2]

When information is withheld from a team, they will fill in the gaps on their own. Based on the limited information available, the team will make assumptions and perceive them as truth. That is a dangerous situation for a team to operate within—because they are often wrong, but never in doubt.

In Chapter 5, one survey respondent wanted the boss to know "That all employees need to be aware of what is going on in the workplace, not just a handful of upper level administrators." Therefore, this chapter's Culture Health Question is: *Is information freely shared by leadership?*

The free flow of information is essential to building a Culture of Transparency necessary for a healthy work environment. In order to make your organization's culture more transparent, consider implementing these three steps.

1. Rethink the risk of transparency.

Be open to reassessing your information policy with your team. Think through the benefits and detriments of withholding the information (Luke 12:2-3). You may well discover that the concerns you had about divulging the information were unfounded. John Mackey and Raj Sisodia explain in *Conscious Capitalism* that "[s]ome companies adopt a compliance mind-set, with limited transparency. They provide information only on a need-to-know basis. By contrast, conscious businesses only withhold information that would be harmful if made public."[3]

> *Look at information like water: it stagnates when it stays in one place.*

Developing transparency will help you prevent your team from developing an active rumor mill. If you can only see the downside of sharing supposedly sensitive information about the company's health, stability, and future, consider what assumptions are being made by your team when they don't have access to that information.

2. Have a policy of inclusion.

Help your team to see issues from other perspectives. Let the information flow help your team see the company from a holistic view. If your organizational structure lends itself to silos, then tear the silos down. Enable information to pass easily from one department to another. Organize your company meetings to facilitate the free flow of information (1 Corinthians 14:26). Encourage collaborative efforts between departments to reduce the barriers to efficient information exchange.

Consider sharing updates about the company with your entire team. These communications should not be just positive news, but also the challenges. The more real you are about how things are going, the more they will think you are sharing all the information available to share.

If your organization is going through significant change, your team will become more prone to make assumptions. There will be fewer stabilizing influences during upheaval and change, and they will be craving more information to understand what's going on. Even though you may have less information available to share, this is a time that you will want to share what little information you have—and do it more often.

If you are forced to downsize, share with the entire team everything that has been happening with the company. Let them know all that you are doing to prevent layoffs. Do not let your team assume layoffs are the first option. Help them to see that is your last resort.

Look at information like water: It stagnates when it stays in one place. Help the information flow in your company, and do not let it stagnate with you or with others.

3. Be prepared for questions.

Even if you implement a policy of openness, you may have times when your team will ask you pointed questions at staff meetings. Do not view those questions as hostile. Most of the time those questions come from a position of uncertainty and fear (1 John 4:18), not from a position of insubordination. Be grateful for those questions, and turn those awkward moments into opportunities to share fully and completely with them.

The real concern is when you get no questions from your team. That signifies that either they don't think they can ask you a question, or—worse—they don't think they can trust your answer. At those times, think through what questions you would have asked if you were in their shoes, and use them as the foundation for updates you can share with the entire team. Most likely others on the team are thinking the same things. That will set the tone for sharing information that will encourage people to ask questions of you.

Even if you are taken off-guard and not prepared to answer the question, say so. Tell your team you will schedule a time when you can answer the question in front of the entire staff. Then after the meeting, go do your research and prepare to answer the question—and the other questions that will result.

As scary as sharing information may be, consider how a greater openness will transform your organizational culture. Be willing to include the entire team in regular communications, and be prepared and available to answer their questions. Help them to see that you are not trying to hide anything. By opening up the information flow, you will enable a transparency between management and employees to change the tenor of all your internal communications.

Reflection Questions

1. When you have new information, what are the risks of sharing it? What are the risks of not sharing it?

2. How can you help information flow better in your workplace?

3. How can you create forums for sharing—and clarifying—information at your company?

Notes
_____

1 Simon Sinek, *Start with Why: How Great Leaders Inspire Everyone to Take Action* (New York: Penguin Group, 2009), 11.

2 Ibid.

3 John Mackey and Raj Sisodia, *Conscious Capitalism: Liberating the Heroic Spirit of Business* (Boston: Harvard Business School Publishing Corporation, 2014), 224.

CHAPTER 30

Meeting Face to Face
Extends Transparency

"For now we see in a mirror dimly, but then face to face.
Now I know in part; then I shall know fully,
even as I have been fully known."

—1 Corinthians 13:12

Moses had the ability to talk with God face to face. He would talk with God just like we would talk with a friend. "When Moses entered the tent, the pillar of cloud would descend and stand at the entrance of the tent, and the LORD would speak with Moses. ... Thus the LORD used to speak to Moses face to face, as a man speaks to his friend" (Exodus 33:9, 11a).

Because Moses was so close with God, he was able to represent God accurately to his fellow Israelites—because he had that transparent face-to-face contact with God.

When we don't have face-to-face contact with others on our team, something gets lost in translation in our interpersonal relations. When we talk with others about attitudes and feelings, only 7 percent of our communications are composed of the words we use. An additional 38 percent of our communications is attributable to how we say it. But a whopping 55 percent of our interpersonal communications is made up of the body language that we use.[1] That face-to-face contact is essential to our understanding each other.

When we don't have in-person communication, we tend to assume that we know what the other is thinking. We can assume the worst when we don't have face-to-face conversations. If we aren't face to face, then we don't see eye to eye.

In the workplace, there can be a reliance on the written word in reports, memos, and emails. They are efficient forms of communication, but something gets lost when we don't communicate in person in presentations, meetings, and conversations. While face-to-face interaction may not always be possible, it should be encouraged as much as possible. In fact, one survey respondent wanted the boss to know "That we need to meet at least once a week so everyone can be on the same page." That's why the Culture Health Question in the final chapter in this section is: *Is information exchanged in person when possible?*

In order to create a Culture of Transparency, it is important to create opportunities for face-to-face interaction among the team.

1. The Importance of Meetings

In our quest for efficiency, business leaders have shunned having meetings for a myriad of reasons: they are time wasters, they get off topic, nothing gets done, etc. I suggest that meetings are not the cause of these problems but actually the *solutions* to these problems *if* they are structured properly.

Patrick Lencioni defends the practice of meeting face to face in *The Advantage*: "No action, activity, or process is more central to a healthy organization than the meeting ... [and] a great deal of the time that leaders spend every day is a result of having to address issues that come about because they aren't being resolved during meetings in the first place."[2]

When people are not spending time with each other, they can assume the worst of each other. Misunderstandings and misinterpretations could be avoided if people would see each other and be able to talk face to face. Many problems could be solved if people actually talked to each other face to face in a regular forum.

> *We can assume the worst when we don't have face-to-face conversations. If we aren't face to face, then we don't see eye to eye.*

Consider how much time is wasted at your company because of misunderstandings. How many misunderstandings could be cleared up through routine interaction?

2. The Purpose of Meetings

Meetings serve a useful purpose in creating culture at an organization—if they are run properly, intentionally, and consistently. Leadership must put thought into how these gatherings can underscore the changes discussed so far in this book and then continue to support that narrative every time they come together.

People crave human interaction. We are relational beings. It behooves a business to have their team meet on a regular basis. The company's employees are indeed the most valuable component of the business. By bringing people together on a regular basis, team leaders can accentuate the importance of the team (Hebrews 10:24-25).

3. The Utility of Meetings

Whenever teams come together in meetings, these are opportunities for emphasizing all the elements discussed so far in Part Two. Leadership can use meetings to showcase a 4T Culture—not in an ostentatious way, but in a way that reinforces all that they are communicating through other means.

- Meetings are excellent venues for giving praise to your team. Staff meetings are also good opportunities for showing how you care. Gathering everyone on the team for training sessions is another reason for having meetings.

- Team meetings are good places to remind everyone of the importance of the organization's vision, values, and purpose. Those concepts should be intertwined into all your company gatherings.

- Being able to run a meeting well can help instill confidence in the team regarding leadership's ability to lead the organization. Meetings give leadership an opportunity for spending time with the team, soliciting their advice, and explaining key decisions.

Face-to-face meetings are important for leadership to share information with the entire team, but they are so much more than that. Meetings are for more than dispensing data; they are forums for demonstrating authenticity, creating clarity, and cultivating understanding.

Reflection Questions

1. How could you use regular and intentional meetings to clear up misunderstandings among your team?

2. How could you use meetings to solidify the team?

3. How could you use meetings to emphasize a 4T Culture?

In Part 2, we have discussed at length a new paradigm for addressing what your employees wish you knew. We have seen how a 4T Culture can resolve the perceptions of insufficient appreciation, inadequate morale, incompetent management, and improper communication. Now we need to take the next step. In Part 3, we will discuss how you can incorporate that paradigm into what you do every day.

Notes

1 Stephen M. R. Covey, *The Speed of Trust: The One Thing That Changes Everything* (New York: Free Press, 2006), 212.

2 Patrick Lencioni, *The Advantage: Why Organizational Health Trumps Everything Else in Business* (San Francisco: Jossey-Bass, 2012), 173, 186.

PART III

BLAZING THE TRAIL

In Part 3, we will explore the means through which you can make significant change in your company by exercising your Active Leadership. In the following chapters, we will identify how you can develop the processes to implement the changes outlined in the Active Leadership paradigm.

Chapter 31: Becoming an Active Leader
> Leadership must actively implement this new paradigm in their workplace culture. It will not automatically happen, and it will not happen overnight. Consistent application of this paradigm will eventually bring this culture to fruition.

Chapter 32: Implementation Step #1 – What You Teach
> Leadership must teach their employees what they want them to know about their culture. Training must be an active component of the workplace. The values that are important to leadership must be actively taught.

Chapter 33: Implementation Step #2 – What You Celebrate
Leadership must recognize, reward, and reinforce the behaviors they want to perpetuate throughout the organization. As a result, your employees will repeat and replicate the behaviors.

Chapter 34: Implementation Step #3 – What You Model
Leadership must personify the change they want to see in their workplace culture. Employees will not buy into the change if leadership is not wholeheartedly committed to it. The change must be seen before it will be copied.

Chapter 35: Implementation Step #4 – What You Permit
Leadership must be serious about follow through. If leadership allows behavior that goes against their core values, then that will undermine all their active efforts to change the culture through teaching, celebrating, and modeling.

Why It Matters

By implementing these intentional steps, you can change how you perceive your role in your workplace and use your newfound influence to effect the change you want to see.

CHAPTER 31

Becoming an Active Leader

"It is not easy to be a pioneer—but oh, it is fascinating!
I would not trade one moment, even the worst moment,
for all the riches in the world."

—Elizabeth Blackwell

Elizabeth Blackwell was a cultural pioneer in the 19th century as the first woman ever to receive a medical degree in the United States. She also became the first woman on the medical register in her native Britain.[1] Being the first woman to enter medical school in the United States, Elizabeth Blackwell was a true pioneer. However, being a pioneer was not easy. Male doctors did not accept her as a peer in the medical profession. People were reluctant to have a female doctor. The path before Elizabeth Blackwell was not trodden. She had to blaze her own trail. But today women doctors—and their patients—can be grateful to her for making the difficult choice of being a leader.

Learning how to change the culture at your organization will not be easy. You will likely not have a path to follow at your company.

You will likely have to blaze your own trail. Your team, however, will be grateful for your making the difficult choice of being a leader.

When Joshua was leading the Israelites into the Promised Land, they were entering an area where idolatry was rampant, child sacrifice was common, and ritual prostitution was the norm. God told them not to do all the all the detestable practices of the nations they were displacing, or else they would be defiled by those practices (Leviticus 18:26-30). As a result, the Israelites had to establish their culture in the land, and not be influenced by the culture of the inhabitants of the land. In sum, God wanted them to be cultural pioneers.

You too will need to be a culture pioneer. As we discussed earlier in the book, business has been stuck in unhealthy leadership models for a long time. Unfortunately, many businesses don't even realize that their leadership models are unhealthy. As a result, they do not realize that their leadership style is causing many of their problems. However, you will be able to demonstrate through the results you get that these principles will work. The more you become an Active Leader, the easier it will be. Changing your thinking and

> *The Active Leadership paradigm will change how you view yourself, your employees, and your company.*

your business processes to fit with the Active Leadership paradigm will take time. The change will not come overnight. Nonetheless, with intentional design and consistent implementation, you will begin to see people at your workplace embrace the changes.

Over the past twenty-five chapters, we have explored in depth what Active Leadership looks like. To review the main components of Active Leadership, below are the four topics discussed in Part Two.

Tenderness

Leadership must care about their team. Team leaders must help their team members believe that they genuinely care about them and take an active and ongoing interest in their professional and personal development. Leadership must regularly give praise for what the team does well and compassionately give constructive feedback to help them improve. Leadership must also place a premium value on flexibility in the workplace and be willing to change.

Team

Leadership must ensure that everyone understands and identifies with the vision of the organization and subscribes to the organization's core values. Leadership must explain the importance of the work that the organization does to the extent that the team members believe that the work they do matters. Everyone must see that their individual performance is important to moving the organization forward and leadership must ensure that everyone feels that all their colleagues are doing their part.

Trust

Leadership must instill in their team members a belief that the leaders know how to run the organization. Leadership must provide sufficient autonomy for assignments and must provide the tools that the team members believe are necessary to do their jobs. Leadership must also ensure that they treat everyone fairly and trust that they will do their best work.

Transparency

Leadership must communicate authentically with team members and ensure that communications are understood by everyone. Leadership must be willing to freely share information—in person as often as practicable—and clarify responsibilities so that everyone understands what is expected.

The Active Leadership paradigm will change how you view yourself, your employees, and your company. Through conscious awareness of these concepts, you will begin to look at things differently. With this new lens, you will be able to redefine your role as a leader, and it will redefine how you view everything else at your company.

As we move into Part Three, we will further explore how to apply these concepts. In the following chapters, you will find a template to design cultural change at your workplace using a strategy composed of these four actions.

What You Teach

Leadership must teach their team what they want them to know about their culture. Training must be an active component of the workplace. The values that are important to leadership must be actively taught.

What You Celebrate

Leadership must recognize, reward, and reinforce the behaviors they want to perpetuate throughout the organization. As a result, the team will repeat and replicate the behaviors.

What You Model

Leadership must personify the change they want to see in their workplace culture. The team will not buy into the change if leadership is not wholeheartedly committed to it. The change must be seen before it will be copied.

What You Permit

Leadership must be serious about follow through. If the leaders allow behavior that goes against their core values, it will undermine all their active efforts to change the culture through teaching, celebrating, and modeling.

Over the next four chapters, we will discuss these four actions and how you can more fully effect the change you want to see in your workplace. As I mentioned before, culture change will require intentionality of design and consistency of implementation over a prolonged period of time.

Business is changing. These principles have been taking root. However, you will still be a pioneer. The trail to be blazed will not be easy, but, as Elizabeth Blackwell said, it will be fascinating. It is my hope and prayer that you will be changed as much through this process as your workplace will be. Someday may you turn around and look upon the trail you have blazed and see how many lives you have transformed because of your efforts.

Reflection Questions

1. Which tenet of the Active Leadership paradigm— Tenderness, Team, Trust, or Transparency—do you find most appealing?

2. Which tenet of Active Leadership do you need to work on the most?

3. How could you be a pioneer for changing the culture at your workplace?

Notes
---

1 Wikipedia, s.v. "Elizabeth Blackwell," last modified August 27, 2017, https://en.wikipedia.org/wiki/Elizabeth_Blackwell.

CHAPTER 32

What You Teach

"Education must not simply teach work—it must teach Life."

—W. E. B. Du Bois

On August 28, 1963, a quarter of a million people from all over the United States gathered on the National Mall in Washington, D.C., to hear Dr. Martin Luther King, Jr. give his "I Have a Dream" speech. In today's age of Twitter-fueled flash mobs, we might not realize how impressive that gathering was. In 1963 there was no internet to organize everyone to attend the speech. No one issued 250,000 invitations to attend the rally. Yet history was made when the Mall was filled with people who came to hear Dr. King.

That crowd did not assemble to hear just anybody. Dr. King had developed a following from faithfully and repeatedly sharing his convictions. Even if they had never heard Dr. King speak before, they knew what they would hear because he had consistently taught the same message over and over again.

Dr. King did not draw a crowd of 250,000 people for the first speech he gave. The Civil Rights movement did not achieve its ends overnight. Leaders like Dr. King had to say the same things over and over again for a long time in order to make the impact they did. It was through teaching that message day in and day out that Dr. King and his contemporaries changed this country.

Dr. King had steadfastly shared the same ideals to the degree that he had become a symbol of the issues that he championed. Similarly, you will not be able to change the culture in your business unless you champion your cause over and over again.

People will not change their views quickly. Your team will not endorse the Active Leadership paradigm just because you talked about it once. They will not want to commit to these principles until they know that you are serious about them. They will bide their time to see if you will continue to talk about these principles. They will want to see that you champion these principles consistently in your workplace.

In Deuteronomy, Moses commanded the Israelites to teach God's laws to their children: when sitting at home, when walking along the road, when getting up in the morning, and when going to sleep. Moses wanted them consistently teaching God's laws at every opportunity so that they would not forget who gave them their prosperity (Deuteronomy 6:6-12).

Similarly, you will need to teach the tenets of Active Leadership to your team at every available opportunity. Explain the approach you will take with them so they will know the approach they should take with customers and suppliers. As an Active Leader, you are teaching all the time. That means everything can be looked at as a teachable opportunity. Here are six opportunities you can use to teach your team.

> *As an Active Leader, you are teaching all the time.*

At staff meetings

When you are with your team at staff meetings, you can remind them of your Active Leadership values of Tenderness, Team, Trust, and Transparency. When you are making decisions, explain how Active Leadership should frame your thinking. As you are thinking through how to serve your customers and how to treat your suppliers and investors, allow these principles to transform the way you work with your employees.

In internal documents

Incorporate the Active Leadership paradigm in your company strategy documents. Allow this thinking to pervade your strategic decision making. Enable your team to understand how their business decisions must fit within this paradigm. Reinforce the Active Leadership values by integrating Tenderness, Team, Trust, and Transparency into your company culture.

In private conversations

As you communicate with your team, sprinkle the concepts of this book into your one-on-one conversations. Let them see that you are consistent in your belief about these principles. Help everyone you talk to realize that you are serious about change and that the Active Leadership paradigm is not just for show. By demonstrating you are just as committed in private as you are in public to these ideals, you will increase your team's belief in your sincerity.

In employee orientation

When new employees come to work with you, use this opportunity to acculturate them to your way of thinking. Introduce them immediately to the commitments you are making to them in terms of how they can expect to be treated at the workplace. While some of your longtime employees may be skeptical of your Active Leadership paradigm, you can prepare new employees to have different expectations. As more new employees are trained in your new culture, they will help to shift the thinking in your workplace.

At exit interviews

When people decide to leave—or you decide it is time for them to leave—include the Active Leadership paradigm tenets in your conversations. If they are leaving on their terms, then encourage them to investigate if their new employer will have Tenderness, Team, Trust and Transparency as operating principles; if they find that their new employer doesn't, you could invite them back. If you have decided it is time for certain employees to leave, then explain to them in what ways they did not fit with the Culture of Tenderness, Team, Trust, and Transparency.

On the walls

If you subscribe to the Active Leadership paradigm enough to change your behavior, then you should be willing to hang it on your walls. Publicly display the values of Tenderness, Team, Trust, and Transparency. Remind everyone at your workplace about your commitment to Active Leadership and your willingness to be held accountable to these principles.

If you consistently teach these principles at every opportunity available to you, eventually you will change the culture at your workplace. It will take intentionality of purpose and it will take consistency of implementation to become part of your culture. But once it is in place, not only will your employees enjoy the workplace more, you will find that the environment is more enjoyable for you as well.

Reflection Questions

1. How can you incorporate the Active Leadership principles into your everyday interactions?

2. How can you include the Active Leadership principles in your written documents?

3. How can you integrate the Active Leadership principles into your company-wide systems?

CHAPTER 33

What You Celebrate

"Celebrate what you want to see more of."

—Tom Peters

In Leviticus, Moses explained the feasts that God wanted the Israelites to celebrate. Moses told them to observe the Passover, the Feast of Firstfruits, the Feast of Weeks, the Feast of Trumpets, the Day of Atonement, and the Feast of Booths. He told them how they were to celebrate each of these special occasions and what time of year they were to celebrate each of them. God wanted the entire nation to celebrate these special days every year in their annual gatherings of corporate worship.

In addition to the feasts, God also told them to institute the Sabbath. He wanted the entire community to rest one day every seven days. The Sabbath day was reserved for rest and corporate worship. Again, everyone in the nation was supposed to celebrate the Sabbath (Leviticus 23).

God gave the Israelites the Passover and the other feasts to remind them of the importance of worship. God instituted these special observances so worship would be part of their national and religious culture. By reserving specific days for celebrations, the Israelites were to remember God in their regular weekly and annual routines. Without those celebrations, God knew they were likely to forget their need for worship and their need for him.

Celebrations are a great way to point out what is important. What the leadership of a country or a company celebrates is what they care about. If your company celebrates when an individual reaches their performance metric goal, then your employees will know their personal performance matters. If your company celebrates what everyone accomplishes together, then they will know that team goals should be pursued. In your company, you can decide what you will celebrate in order to implement the Active Leadership paradigm. As the business leadership writer Tom Peters said, "Celebrate what you want to see more of."

Reaching major personal or team goals don't have to be the only occasions to celebrate. Celebrations don't have to be big affairs. You can use little things to change the culture in your workplace. All you have to do is follow these 3 R's.

1. Recognize

To begin to change your workplace culture, first consider how you want to implement the values of Tenderness, Team, Trust, and Transparency in your workplace. Then take stock of where you are now. You can use the Active Leadership Diagnostic Tool in Appendix B to assess where you are strong and where you need improvement. (If you need assistance from a third party to independently assess how you are doing, contact us at info@transformationalimpactllc.com.)

Once you have an idea of what needs to change, then you will know what kinds of behaviors you want to encourage. When you see behavior that demonstrates the Active Leadership tenets, go out of your way to recognize that behavior. Not only should you make a mental note of what they did, but make sure that the person who did it knows you recognized it. Perhaps you saw them giving constructive feedback to a colleague or a direct report. Or perhaps you learned how someone served the company or a customer beyond the call of duty. Take the opportunity right when you learn about it to congratulate them for their exemplary service in connection with the company's values.

2. Reward
When you recognize the behavior, then be sure to reward it. Make sure that you do something positive and memorable in response. Whatever is rewarded will be repeated. The reward doesn't have to be complicated. It can be as simple as smiling when you see someone doing something you want replicated. You can also compliment them on what they did. Just taking the time to notice that they did something that was meaningful to you can go a long way. If appropriate, you can give a special reward. This could be special company perks, a cash bonus, a gift card to a favorite store, a vacation getaway to an exotic location, or time away from the workplace. The key is it should be something of significant value to the recipient.

3. Reinforce
The way to make positive behaviors repeated by everyone else at your workplace is to reinforce that behavior in front of everyone else there. That way you gain the benefit of encouraging among the entire team the behaviors you have seen exhibited by a limited number of people. When the team is at an all-staff meeting, go out of your way to recognize and reward people who have exhibited those positive behaviors. You can reinforce their behavior by complimenting them in front of everyone else. Or you can honor them by presenting their reward to them in front of the entire group. Whatever it is,

the incentive must be meaningful to everyone in the group.

Don't underestimate the power of the spoken word. As an Active Leader, your words have more power than you realize to change the culture around you. Even if you don't have a large budget for rewards, you can still reinforce desired behaviors by acknowledging them in private and in public. People want to be recognized and rewarded—and they want to be recognized and rewarded by *you*. If you reward their positive behaviors, they will repeatedly respond in the way that you want them to. And if you reinforce their behaviors in front of the entire team, then the whole team will do them as well. As a result, you will change the culture in your workplace.

> *As an Active Leader, your words have more power than you realize to change the culture around you.*

Reflection Questions

1. How could you recognize positive behaviors in your workplace?

2. In what creative ways could you reward those behaviors?

3. How could you implement a regular process of reinforcing those behaviors in front of the team?

CHAPTER 34

What You Model

"Each person must live their life as a model for others."

—Rosa Parks

The apostle Paul understood the importance of modeling. He realized that how he conducted his life would have an impact on how others lived their lives. He told the Philippians: "What you have learned and received and heard and seen in me—practice these things" (Philippians 4:9). He knew he had to live in such a way that others could do what he did and grow closer to God as a result.

In addition, Paul understood the impact of the lives he had touched. Paul realized that how they lived their lives would be a reflection of his leadership. More importantly, how they lived their lives would influence more people than he personally could. Paul told the Corinthians: "You yourselves are our letter of recommendation, written on our hearts, to be known and read by all. And you show that you are a letter from Christ delivered by us, written not with ink but with the Spirit of the living God, not on tablets of stone but on tablets of human hearts" (2 Corinthians 3:2-3). Paul knew he had to set the

201

tone and influence those he could reach through the power of the Holy Spirit; then he could let them continue to perpetuate his teachings by how they lived their lives and influenced those around them.

As a leader, how you interact with the people on your team is extremely important. In fact, your Active Leadership is more important than you may realize. Everyone in your charge is constantly watching you. Your team will pick up more of what is important to you by your actions than by your words. In fact, people may not be able to hear what you say because your actions will speak more loudly. As the leader, you set the tone: You will need to model the behavior you expect to see in your company.

1. Be the leader you would want to follow.
As the leader, you set the example for your organization. What you do, others will replicate. You will make the greatest impact as a leader when you want the best for your team. When you choose to lead by looking out for the best interests of those on your team, you will garner attention from your team. When you demonstrate that intentional servant attitude day after day and week after week, your team will see how they could be like that as well.

By being willing to demonstrate a 4T Culture at your workplace, you can show those around you how it can be done. They will know it is possible because they will see you do it. Over time, people will start to act like you act because they will see it's a better way, but only because they saw you do it first.

2. Live by your standards.
You cannot just tell your team what you want them to do. You have to live it as well. Whatever codes of conduct you apply to the team must also apply to you. You set the standard of what is acceptable behavior, and you have to live by your own rules. When you commit

to do things, you must follow up on those commitments. You can set the standard, but you then must consistently abide by what you have said—or else you will cause widespread mistrust.

You cannot just tell your team what you want them to do. You have to live it as well.

The easiest way to build trust with others is to do what you say you will do. The hardest way to build trust with others is also to do what you say you will do. Your actions have to be consistently implemented with your team. It can take a long time to earn the trust of your team—but you can lose it in a moment. If you do not follow up on your commitments, then your team will think you have broken faith with them. Hypocrisy will destroy any credibility you have with your team, and it will be even harder to restore broken trust.

3. Admit your mistakes.

There may be times that you will fall down in your responsibilities. You may fail your team in your commitments. That's why you have to admit your mistakes. You will not always live up to your own values, and you need to be ready to acknowledge that and take responsibility for it when you do. Don't deceive yourself into thinking that people don't notice when you have a misstep. Reinforcing your Active Leadership is more important than saving face in front of your team. In fact, they will respect you more if you do not try to hide your infractions.

When you are under pressure is when your true colors will show. That's when your team will be watching you more closely than ever. They want to see if your Active Leadership is just a lot of talk or if you really mean it. If you consistently live it, they will want to follow you more. When you can consistently convey your values—in what you do and not just what you say—you will be more attractive as a leader and your team will be more interested in what you have to say.

Leaders who habitually try to hide their mistakes or shift the blame for what they did wrong will never be able to build trust with their team. Humility is a key ingredient for trustworthiness. When you mess up, you must fess up. It is only through a sincere, heartfelt apology that you can reconstruct the foundation of trust.

Don't just talk about Active Leadership; live it in front of everyone. Be the leader and show everyone by your actions how you are serious about the changes to your company culture. If you mess up, be quick to admit it, and keep moving forward. You don't have to be perfect: You just have to model the standard you want to see in others.

Reflection Questions

1. What kind of leaders have you been inspired to follow? How can you be more like them?

2. How can you more intentionally incorporate your standards into how you live every day?

3. How do you handle making mistakes? Do you try to hide them? Or do you admit them?

CHAPTER 35

What You Permit

*"People are going to behave however
the social norms permit, and beyond that."*

—Max Cannon

In his first letter to the Corinthians, Paul rebuked them for their lax attitude toward one of the members of the church in Corinth. One of the church members was having sexual relations with his father's wife, and the church there was doing nothing about it (1 Corinthians 5:1). Paul gave them direct instructions on how they should address this situation, so that two things would happen. First, this man would realize that his conduct did not conform to God's standard. Second, the others in the church would realize this conduct did not conform to God's standard.

Paul realized that he had to address this issue head on. He could not pretend that it wasn't happening or assume that it would get worked out. He had to stop the behavior before it spread. Paul instructed the Corinthians, "Do you not know that a little leaven leavens the whole lump [of dough]? Cleanse out the old leaven that you may be a new lump"

(1 Corinthians 5:6-7). Whatever gets permitted gets perpetuated.

Like what Paul experienced with the Corinthians, something can creep into your culture without you realizing it. You may have done all you can to teach, celebrate, and model your Active Leadership paradigm, but it can be undone by what you permit. Living the Active Leadership paradigm requires intentionality in design. It also requires consistency in implementation. Your team will mimic your behavior, but they will also do what you permit. If you condone certain behavior that goes

> *Living the Active Leadership paradigm requires intentionality in design. It also requires consistency in implementation.*

against your core values, then people will replicate that behavior. What you permit has the same effect as what you teach, celebrate, and model.

Management fads come and go. If the boss repeatedly changes his mind about how he wants to organize the workplace, then no one will commit to learning the new system. Instead, they will bide their time and wait to see what he will decide to do next. They are not being rebellious; they just want to know that the boss is serious. Change is hard, and they will not go out of their way if everything changes all over again in the near future.

Many bosses say what they want the team to do, but their team members don't think they mean what they say. People don't always do what you *expect*. They do what you *inspect*. People will choose the path of least resistance, so your company culture will be created by whatever environment predominates. Here's how you can make sure that the 4 T's take hold.

1. Stay vigilant

Stay committed to implementing the Active Leadership paradigm (2 Thessalonians 3:13). When you feel like you have been talking about it *ad nauseum*, your team will probably have just started paying attention. Keep on talking about it. They will eventually catch on.

When you feel that you have highlighted the changes you want to make—and yet you still see behavior that goes against the Active Leadership paradigm—keep rewarding and reinforcing the right behaviors. People will eventually notice.

When you feel that you have modeled these principles and yet no one seems to notice, realize it may take time for them to recognize the change in your behavior. Even if they do see the change in you, they may be watching you to make sure that this is a real change. Don't lose heart. You will win them over in time. Change does not come easily. Know that you're doing the right thing for the right reason. Eventually you will see the results you want.

2. Take your temperature

Periodically assess how your culture is changing. You can have your employees participate in an anonymous survey to see how their attitudes are changing based on the changes you have made. You can use the Active Leadership Diagnostic Tool in Appendix B as a template to use with your team on an annual basis. (If you need help to administer the survey, you will find additional resources at www.WhatYourEmployeesWishYouKnew.com.)

Over time you will see incremental changes in the attitudes of your team. Seeing those changes in your survey results will be encouraging to you. Sharing the survey results with your team will be enlightening to them as well. Those results will help them see that their colleagues believe that the situation is changing and will encourage them to want to become part of the change too.

3. Don't go it alone

Don't feel like you have to go it alone. Share this book with a colleague or a fellow business owner and implement these changes together. Set up a time to meet together regularly, even if it's only by conference call. Encourage each other when it gets tough. Share ideas with each other about what has been working. Hold each other accountable to stick with it. You can even form a group with other business owners or managers who want to implement these ideas. Form a Mastermind group with others who want to see their company cultures change. Go through this book together, and help each other get through the process.

Remember: it will take months before you see any results from the change. Don't let that dissuade you. You know this is the right course of action, and your people will eventually enjoy the change. As the apostle Paul writes, "let us not grow weary of doing good, for in due season we will reap, if we do not give up" (Galatians 6:9).

The American workplace is a mess, and the prevailing leadership thinking has produced the mess. If you always do what you have always done, then you will always get what you have always gotten. There is a better way, and you have the power within your hands to make that change.

Reflection Questions

1. What systems can you put in place to remind you to continue to talk about Active Leadership?

2. How can you incorporate regular assessment of your Active Leadership into your company calendar?

3. Who could you ask to walk alongside you as you implement Active Leadership in your company?

Conclusion

"In every day, there are 1,440 minutes.
That means we have 1,440 daily opportunities
to make a positive impact."

—Les Brown

Early in the morning, a boy walked along the beach. He moved quickly with a sense of purpose, as if looking for something. Occasionally he would stop and grab something from the sand and throw it into the ocean.

Walking from the opposite direction was another boy. He meandered along, occasionally finding something in the sand and putting it in his pocket. The second boy asked the first boy if he wanted to play.

"Too busy," said the first boy.

"Doing what," asked the second boy.

"I'm looking for starfish."

"What for?"

"I'm taking the ones washed up on the beach that are still alive and throwing them in the water."

"What a waste of time. You can't possibly pick up all the starfish on this beach. There must be hundreds of them—thousands of them."

"So?" asked the first boy.

"So what you're doing can't possibly make a difference for all those starfish!"

The first boy picked up a starfish and threw it in the ocean. "It mattered to that one."

It's true that the first boy couldn't save *all* the starfish on that beach, but he had a big impact on *some*. You can't change the state of the American workplace, but you can change the culture in *your* workplace. Don't focus on what you can't do, but focus on what you can do.

For those who work for you, you can make a huge impact in their lives. You can impact how they view your company. You can affect how they feel about the work they do. You can change how they feel about themselves. You can make a profound impact.

Ultimately what you do every day is not about making a living. It's about making a life. You can do more than just make money. You can make a difference. Your company can bring out the best in everyone around you. Your workplace can have a positive effect on your employees, your customers, your suppliers, your investors, and your community. You can put your Active Leadership values into action and produce a transformational culture. As a result, your business will have a triple bottom-line impact. Here are the three bottom-line benefits of having a 4T Culture at your workplace.

1. Social Bottom Line

Your team will feel more empowered to make the company better because you will be treating them the way you would want to be treated (Matthew 7:12). As a result, they will serve your customers better, which will spill over into the community. You will have more influence where you live and work because your good reputation will precede you.

Through living your Active Leadership values, you will foster greater employee engagement. Your employees will sense they are valued and their work is appreciated. Your team will know that you care about them not only as workers but as people. They will feel the work the company does matters and what they do personally matters. They will feel equipped, empowered, and entrusted to do good work. They will feel that they are listened to and they are understood. Your team will believe more in your

> *You can do more than just make money. You can make a difference.*

company, go the extra mile for others, and have more joy in their work because you are willing to show them that you love them as you would love yourself (Leviticus 19:18; Matthew 22:39; Mark 12:31; Romans 13:8-10; Galatians 5:14).

How you treat your employees will have a ripple effect on their families. Your employees will see themselves differently, and as a result they will see their families differently. The Active Leadership your employees see in you will show them how they can treat their families as well.

2. Economic Bottom Line
When you treat your team the way you would want to be treated (Matthew 7:12), then they will treat your customers the way they would want to be treated. As a result, you will have a more profitable bottom line.

Your customers will feel good about their interactions with your company because your Active Leadership values will show through your team. That will enhance your brand and develop deeper customer trust. Because your customers will feel increased value from their business with you, you will retain more customers and possibly be able to charge more for your product or service. As a result, you will make more money.

Treating your team the way you would want to be treated will affect your suppliers too. Your team will see your suppliers in a new way and will treat them differently. As a result, your suppliers will be more willing to work with you even if you come upon hard times. If you started treating your investors with the same Active Leadership paradigm, think how that would impact your relationship with them: They would give you the benefit of the doubt more often and they would be more likely to stay with you—even during hard times.

By intentionally creating a culture where you live your Active Leadership paradigm, you will make more money because you will be creating an environment where you live what you believe.

3. Spiritual Bottom Line
The people who regularly work with you will be watching. They will be curious to see if you will live your Active Leadership consistently. They want to see if you mean what you say. If your actions back up your words, they will be inspired to learn more about your faith. By living your Active Leadership daily, you can reach people with the Gospel in a way that a church cannot do. A church has the attention of people for a portion of only one day a week. Your team will see you living the words of Jesus every day at work.

People in your community will see something different in you because of the way your employees and customers talk about you. Your community will notice how you treat your employees, your suppliers, your investors, and your customers. When you intentionally and consistently love your neighbor, your community will notice.

By intentionally designing your culture based on Tenderness, Team, Trust, and Transparency—and consistently living it—your company will have a transformational effect on people. You will be able to build your people, enhance your profitability, and impact your community. As a result, your company will have a triple bottom-line impact.

The biggest impact that the Active Leadership paradigm will have is on *you*. You will see yourself as a catalyst for change that you may never have seen before. And you will see the impact you can have—because you were willing to act on what your employees wish you knew.

Reflection Questions

1. What results do you aspire to achieve in your social bottom line?

2. What results do you aspire to achieve in your economic bottom line?

3. What results do you aspire to achieve in your spiritual bottom line?

APPENDIX A

Additional Research Questions and Findings

Below are the additional questions and the aggregated responses from the survey conducted by WPA Opinion Research (referenced in Chapter 1).

Including yourself, what is the total number of people currently living in your household?

One	20%
Two	34%
Three or more	46%

Are there children in your household under the age of eighteen?

Yes	35%
No	65%

What was the last grade in school you completed?

High school graduate or less	32%
Some college	31%
College graduate or higher	37%

Was your TOTAL household income BEFORE taxes for 2015:

Less than $35,000	28%
$35,000 to less than $50,000	12%
$50,000 to less than $75,000	19%
$75,000 to less than $100,000	17%
$100,000 or more	24%

Which of the following describes your race?

White	61%
Hispanic, Mexican, Latino, Spanish	18%
African-American	12%
Other	9%

What is your age?

18-34	34%
35-44	22%
45-54	22%
55-64	16%
65 or over	6%

What is your gender?

Male	54%
Female	46%

Region:

Northeast	20%
Midwest	23%
South	35%
West	22%

APPENDIX B

Active Leadership Diagnostic Tool

You can use these 20 questions as a self-diagnostic tool for your company. On a scale of 0-5 with 0 being *not at all* and 5 being *the best possible*, rate the culture at your company.

Answer these questions as honestly as you can. Consider having your entire team also take this survey and give you their answers anonymously. If you need assistance with assessing your company's cultural health, you can avail yourself of additional resources at www.WhatYourEmployeesWishYouKnew.com.

Tenderness

_____ 1. Do employees believe that leadership genuinely cares about them?

_____ 2. Do employees believe leadership takes an active and ongoing interest in their professional and personal development?

_____ 3. Does the workplace allow for flexibility to deal with the demands of the situation?

_____ 4. Does leadership regularly give praise for what employees do well?

_____ 5. Does leadership compassionately give constructive feedback to help employees improve?

Team

_____ 1. Does everyone understand and identify with the vision of the organization?

_____ 2. Does everyone subscribe to the organization's values?

_____ 3. Does everyone believe the organization's work matters?

_____ 4. Do employees believe their individual performance is necessary to move the organization forward?

_____ 5. Do employees feel that their colleagues are pulling their full weight?

Trust

_____ 1. Has leadership provided the tools that employees believe are necessary to do the job?

_____ 2. Do employees have confidence that leadership knows how to run the organization?

_____ 3. Do employees believe that leadership treats everyone fairly?

_____ 4. Does leadership provide sufficient autonomy for assignments so workers can take initiative in their work?

_____ 5. Do employees believe that leadership trusts them to produce a good work product?

Transparency

_____ 1. Do employees believe that leadership consistently communicates in an authentic manner?

_____ 2. Have expectations been clarified so that everyone understands their responsibilities?

_____ 3. Are communications between leadership and employees characterized by mutual understanding?

_____ 4. Is information freely shared by leadership?

_____ 5. Is information exchanged in person when possible?

About the Author

Robert McFarland is a leadership consultant, executive coach, and conference speaker. Robert has worked with myriad organizations conducting strategic planning, providing branding guidance, and giving communications counsel.

Robert is President of Transformational Impact LLC, a leadership development consultancy helping companies envision their preferred future, map the strategy to get there, and create the company culture to bring it to fruition. After serving evangelical ministries and nonprofits for 20 years as an executive, board member, and consultant, Robert founded Transformational Impact LLC to help for-profit companies and nonprofits capitalize on the power of their vision.

Robert enjoys helping people change their thinking, so they can get the results they want at work and in life. His Impactful Lives blog at www.RobertMcFarland.net focuses on how intentional Christians can lead their thinking in their spiritual lives and in their professional lives to lead impactful lives.

Robert serves as the Intentional Leadership Coach for the Intentional Living Center and is a frequent contributor to the Intentional Living broadcast and features. He is a member of the Board of Directors of the National Religious Broadcasters and the Chairman of the Board of Directors of The Family Foundation of Virginia.

Robert and his wife, Tamitha, recently moved their six children out of the Washington, D.C. area to the Shenandoah Valley of Virginia, where they now wake up to the sound of cows instead of cars.

Made in the USA
Middletown, DE
17 February 2019